Classic Kata of Shorinji Ryu

Okinawan Karate Forms of Richard 'Biggie' Kim

Leroy Rodrigues

authorHOUSE®

AuthorHouse™ LLC
1663 Liberty Drive
Bloomington, IN 47403
www.authorhouse.com
Phone: 1-800-839-8640

Published by AuthorHouse   03/15/2014

ISBN: 978-1-4918-6525-5 (sc)
ISBN: 978-1-4918-6524-8 (e)

Library of Congress Control Number: 2014903259

Contents

Appendix

Contributors:

Nobu Kaji – all art work, sketches, cover design, image layout, Japanese language labeling, and research.

Bernardo Mercado – photography, text content, book layout, editing and project management.

Kathleen Flaherty & Jose Novoa – proof reading.

Chapter One
Introduction

I believe that kata is one of the most important components of martial arts, yet perhaps the least appreciated by many. I often tell my students that kata is the encyclopedia of any karate system. Kata also allows us to practice karate basics and to stay in good physical condition. A partner is not required or any special space to practice kata. As we age, our bodies cannot take the punishment involved in other combat arts like boxing, kick boxing, wrestling and judo. Kata can be practiced into old age and self-defense capabilities can be maintained throughout one's life.

Kata has two types of techniques, those that can easily be ascertained by watching a kata, and others referred to as hidden techniques. Hidden techniques can be multiple for every overt technique. In other words, hidden techniques are as varied as the instructors who derive or extract them from the kata. That is why kata is endlessly interesting and challenging.

Kata is supposed to be combat against imaginary opponents. Kata must be performed so the subjective experience of the practitioner and that of an outside observer feels and looks like the performance is real combat. Therefore, proper focus, timing, mental attitude, power, and, of course, proper technique, must always be present.

Kata in Okinawa was used to disguise the practice of self-defense during the Shimazu Invasion of the Ryukyu Kingdom in 1609, when occupiers outlawed martial arts practice by the native people. This meant that Okinawans could practice their martial arts in full view of law enforcement without raising any suspicion. To the uninitiated, kata looked like harmless dancing that posed no threat to the overlords.

Richard 'Biggie' Kim, Lefty Nakayama, Clarence Lee, Richard Lee, and Herbert Lee taught me all the katas contained in this book. These katas are very rare and only a few people around the world practice them. That is the reason why I decided to document and share these kata. I felt an obligation to not allow these beautiful and effective forms to be lost to history.

In a sense, this is a tribute to Richard 'Biggie' Kim, one of the most knowledgeable martial artists the world has ever known. Please be aware that this book is meant for high level traditional martial artists and for those who already are familiar with these katas. It is a refresher, so to speak. As with any kata, they cannot be properly learned from a book.

安南拳

ANANKU

Chapter Two
Ananku

Alternate names: Ananko, Annan

Meaning of kata name: southern country fist

From whom the author learned kata: Richard 'Biggie' Kim

Lineage and history of kata:

Originally, Ananku came from Chotoku Kyan (1870-1945) who traveled to Taiwan in 1922 for a karate demonstration. There he trained and studied with local Taiwanese martial artists and created this Kata.

Chotoku Kyan trained under various Okinawan masters including Sokon Matsumura (Shuri-te, 1809-1899), Anko Azato (Shuri-te, 1828-1944), Kosaku Matsumora (Tomari-te, 1829-1898), Koukan Oyadomari (1827-1905) and Gicho Maeda Pechin (Tomari-te, 1826-1890), also his father Chofu Kyan.

1.
Yoi

6.
Hidari Zenkutsu-Dachi
Hidari Uchi-Uke

(step forward with left foot)

2.
Kamae

7.
Migi Gyaku-Zuki

3.
Hidari-Koukutsu-Dachi
Hidari Shuto-Uke

(step forward with left foot)

8.
Hidari Oi-Zuki

4.
Migi-Koukutsu-Dachi
Migi Shuto-Uke

(step forward with right foot)

9.
Migi-Shizen-Tai

(turn clockwise)

5.
Hidari Shizen-Tai

(look to left)

10.
Migi Zenkutsu-Dachi
Migi Uchi-Uke

(step forward with right foot)

11.
Migi Zenkutsu-Dachi
Hidari Gyaku-Zuki

16.
Migi Sanchin-Dachi
Morote-Hira-Nukite

12.
Migi Zenkutsu-Dachi
Migi Oi-Zuki

17.
Migi Sanchin-Dachi
Ryo-ken Koshi

13.
Morote Jodan Hasami-Uke

(turn counter clockwise,
and stand straight up, heels up,
elbows and fists together)

18.
Migi Sanchin-Dachi
Morote-Shita-Zuki

(slide step, right foot first
and left foot)

14.
Migi Sanchin-Dachi
Morote Gedan-Barai

(turn right)

19. (Kiai)
Migi Zenkutsu-Dachi
Migi Oi-Zuki

(step forward with right foot)

15.
Migi Sanchin-Dachi
Morote Kaishu Soto-Uke

20.
Hidari Zenkutsu-Dachi
Hidari Uchi-Uke

(step forward with left foot to
left front 45 degree)

21.
Hidari Zenkutsu-Dachi
Migi Gyaku-Zuki

24.
(Kiai)
Hidari Zenkutsu-Dachi
Migi Hiji-Uchi

22.
Hidari Zenkutsu-Dachi
Migi Oi-Zuki

25.
Migi Zenkutsu-Dachi
Migi Uchi-Uke

(turn right 90 degree)

23a.
Migi Mae-Geri

(chamber)

26.
Migi Zenkutsu-Dachi
Hidari Gyaku-Zuki

23b.
Migi Mae-Geri

(snap kick)

27.
Migi Oi-Zuki

23c.
Migi Mae-Geri

(chamber)

28.
(Kiai)
Hidari Hiji-Uchi

29.
Migi Kasei-Zenkutsu-Dachi
Hidari Gedan,
Migi Jodan-Uke

(step forward with right foot
and turn back)

32.
(front view)

29.
(side view)

33.
Hidari Kousa-Dachi
Migi Uchi-Uke Gamae

(put the right foot down and
step left foot front, keep the
right inside block)

30.
Migi Zenkutsu-Dachi
Migi Oi-Zuki

(step forward with right foot)

33.
(front view)

31.
Migi Uchi-Uke

34.
Migi Mae-Geri

(keep the right inside block)

32.
Migi Hiza-Uke
Migi Uchi-Uke-Gamae

(keep the right inside block)

35.
Migi Zenkutsu-Dachi
Migi Gedan Ura-Ken

35.
(front view)

40.
Yame

36.
Migi Zenkutsu-Dachi
Migi Jyodan Ura-Ken

41.
Kiotsuke

37. (Kiai)
Hidari Gyaku-Zuki

42.
Rei

38.
Hidari Kokutsu-Dachi
Hidari Shuto-Uke

(turn around counter clockwise
180 degree)

43.
Naore

39.
Migi Kokutsu-Dachi
Migi Shuto-Uke

(step back with left foot)

JYUROKU

Chapter Three
Jyuroku

Alternate name: Juroku

Meaning of kata name: sixteen

From whom the author learned kata: Richard Lee

Lineage and history of kata: Shito-Ryu

Jyuroku was created by Kenwa Mabuni (founder of Shito-Ryu, 1889-1952) in 1941, and named the kata "16" because of the year 16 of the Showa era (1926-1989) of Japan.

1.
Yoi

6.
Hidari Zenkutsu-Dachi
Hidari Haishu-Uke

(step forward with left foot)

2.
Kamae

7.
Migi Zenkutsu-Dachi
Hidari Nagashi-Uke
Migi Chudan Oi-Zuki

(step forward with right foot)

3.
Hidari Zenkutsu-Dachi
Migi Chudan-Zuki

(step left foot to left)

8.
Gyaku-Zenkutsu-Dachi
Hidari Shotei-Age-Uke
Migi Shotei-Gedan-Uke

(shift to reverse front stance)

4.
Kiba-Dachi
Hidari Chudan-Zuki

(shift to right)

9.
Migi Kokutsu-Dachi
Migi Shuto-Uke

(step back with right foot,
to back 45 degree to right)

5.
Kiba-Dachi
Migi Chudan-Zuki

10.
(step forward with left foot)
Hidari Kokutsu-Dachi
Hidari Shuto-Uke

11.
Hidari Zenkutsu-Dachi
Morote Shotei-Zuki

15a.
(front view)

12.
Migi Kokutsu-Dachi
Migi Shuto-Uke

(step forward with right foot
to left 45 degree)

16a.
Migi Chudan Mae-Geri

(chamber)

13.
Hidari Kokutsu-Dachi
Hidari Shuto-Uke

(step forward with left foot)

16b.
Migi Chudan Mae-Geri

(snap kick)

14.
Hidari Zenkutsu-Dachi
Morote Shotei-Zuki

16c.
Migi Chudan Mae-Geri

(chamber)

15.
Hidari Zenkutsu-Dachi
Migi Chudan-Zuki

(look to right)

17.
Migi Zenkutsu-Dachi
Hidari Gyaku-Zuki

18.
Migi Zenkutsu-Dachi
Hidari Uchi-Uke

21.
Hidari Zenkutsu-Dachi
Migi Uchi-Uke

19a.
Hidari Chudan Mae-Geri

(chamber)

22a.
Migi Mae-Geri

(chamber)

19b.
Hidari Chudan Mae-Geri

(snap kick)

22b.
Migi Mae-Geri

(snap kick)

19c.
Hidari Chudan Mae-Geri

(chamber)

22c.
Migi Mae-Geri

(chamber)

20.
Hidari Zenkutsu-Dachi
Migi Gyaku-Zuki

(step forward with left foot)

24.
Migi Zenkutsu-Dachi
Morote Jodan-Uke

(step forward with right foot)

20

25.
Moroto Jodan-Uke

(half step in with left foot)

30.
Migi Kokutsu-Dachi
Migi Morote Ude-Uke

(step forward with right foot)

26.
Migi Zenkutsu-Dachi
Morote Uraken-Uchi

(step forward with right foot)

31.
Migi Kosa-Dachi
Hidari Kaishu-Uke

(shift to right, left foot behind
right foot)

27.
Hidari Kokutsu-Dachi
Hidari Morote Ude-Uke

(turn around to left)

32.
(keep the left open hand block,
and move left foot forward
slowly)

28.
Migi Kokutsu-Dachi
Migi Morote Ude-Uke

(step forward with right foot)

33.
(Kiai)
Hidari Sagi-Ashi-Dachi
Migi Ude-Uke
Higari Soe-Te-Uke

(right foot behind left knee)

29.
Hidari Kokutsu-Dachi
Hidari Morote Ude-Uke

(look to left, step out with
left foot)

34.
Migi Mae-Geri

(snap kick, keep the right
forearm block)

35.
Migi Hiza-Uke

(keep the right forearm block)

40.
Morote Shotei-Uke

(right hand up, left hand down)

36.
Hidari Zenkutsu-Dachi
Hidari Shotei-Zuki

(move right foot back)

41.
Morote Shotei-Uke

(turn both hands clockwise and
left hand up, right hand down
and push down)

37.
Hidari Zenkutsu-Dachi
Migi Chudan Gyaku-Zuki

42.
Yame

38.
Hidari Zenkutsu-Dachi
Hidari Chudan Oi-Zuki

43.
Naore

39.
(left foot back to right foot,
stand straight, heel together,
left fist over right fist)

心波初段

Shinpa-Shodan

Chapter Four
Shinpa Shodan

Alternate names: Shimpa-1, Shinpa-1

Meaning of kata name: wave of mind or wave from heart

From whom the author learned kata: Richard 'Biggie' Kim

Lineage and history of kata: Naha-Te (Uechi-Ryu)

Shinpa Shodan was named by Kenwa Mabuni in the early 40's as Jyuroku. He learned Simpa-1 and Simpa-2 from Kanbun Uechi (1877-1948) when he was in Osaka Japan (1910-1948). The two Shinpa Kata are pieces of Uechi's version of Supa-rinpei (108 steps), which Uechi did not completely learn when he was in Fikien, China under a Chinese Tiger-Fist master named Shushiwa.

1.
Yoi

6.
(right fist meets left open hand at front)

2.
Kamae

(left foot in, heel together, hand at side)

7.
Hidari Kokutsu-Dachi
Hidari Shuto-Uke

(step forward with left foot)

3.
(hands at straight front)

8.
Left Zenkutsu-Dachi
Migi Gyaku-Zuki

(shift to front stance)

4.
(palms down)

9.
Migi Kokutsu-Dachi
Migi Shuto-Uke

(step forward with right foot)

5.
(hands straight to the side)

10.
Migi Zenkutsu-Dachi
Hidari Gyaku-Zuki

(shift to front stance)

11.
Hidari Kokutsu-Dachi
Hidari Shuto-Uke

(step forward with left foot)

15b.
Migi Mae-Geri

(snap kick)

12.
Hidari Zenkutsu-Dachi
Migi Gyaku-Zuki

(shift to front stance)

15c.
Migi Mae-Geri

(chamber)

13.
Hidari Zenkutsu-Dachi
Hidari Oi-Zuki

16.
Hidari Kokutsu-Dachi
Hidari Shuto-Uke

(put right foot down and turn
to left, then step forward with
left foot)

14.
Hidari Zenkutsu-Dachi
Migi Gyaku-Zuki

19.
Migi Zenkutsu-Dachi
Migi Hiji-Ate

(step forward with right foot)

15a.
Migi Mae-Geri

(chamber)

20.
Hidari Kokutsu-Dachi
Hidari Shuto-Uke

(turn counter clockwise
180 degree)

21.
Hidari Zenkutsu-Dachi
Migi Gyaku-Zuki

26.
Hidari Zenkutsu-Dachi
Hidari Oi-Zuki

22.
Migi Kokutsu-Dachi
Migi Shuto-Uke

(step forward with right foot)

27.
Hidari Zenkutsu-Dachi
Migi Gyaku-Zuki

23.
Migi Zenkutsu-Dachi
Hidari Gyaku-Zuki

(shift to front stance)

28a.
Migi Mae-Geri

(chamber)

24.
Hidari Kokutsu-Dachi
Hidari Shoto-Uke

(step forward with left foot)

28b.
Migi Mae-Geri

(snap kick)

25.
Hidari Zenkutsu-Dachi
Migi Gyaku-Zuki

(shift to front stance)

28c.
Migi Mae-Geri

(chamber)

28

29.
(keep right punch, put right foot down slowly)

34.
Hidari Kokutsu-Dachi
Hidari Shuto-Uke

(turn back counter clockwise)

30.
Migi Kokutsu-Dachi
Migi Shuto-Uke

(step back with left foot, move Shuto-Uke slow with dynamic tension)

35.
Hidari Shizen-Tai
Morote Jodan- Shuto Gamae

(move up, stand straight)

31.
Migi Kasei-Zenkutsu-Dachi
Hidari Gedan,
Migi Jodan-Uke

(turn back counter clockwise)

36.
Hidari Shizen-Tai
Morote Jodan- Shuto Gamae

(move right toes back)

32a.
(half step in with right foot, look front)

37.
Hidari Shizen-Tai
Morote Jodan- Shuto Gamae

(move right heel back, and left foot slides back at the same time)

32b.
Migi Kokutsu-Dachi
Migi Morote Ude-Uke

(step forward with right foot)

38.
Hidari Shizen-Tai
Morote Jodan- Shuto Gamae

(move right toes back)

39.
Hidari Shizen-Tai
Morote Jodan- Shuto
Gamae

(move right heel back,
and left foot slides back
at the same time)

40.
Hidari Kokutsu-Dachi
Jodan Shuto Kosa-Uke

(slide step forward left foot and
right foot)

41.
Hidari Kokutsu-Dachi
Morote Shita-Zuki

(slide step forward left foot and
right foot)

41a.
(front view)

42.
Migi Kokutsu-Dachi
Migi Ryoken Gamae

(turn around clockwise 180'
degree, face front)

43.
Hidari Kokutsu-Dachi
Hidari Ryoken Gamae

(step forward with left foot)

44.
Migi Kokutsu-Dachi
Migi Ryoken Gamae

(step forward with right foot)

45.
Morote Kaishu-Gamae

(move right toes and left toes
back at same time,
both hands open as shuto)

46.
Morote Kaishu-Gamae

(move right heel and left heel
back at same time,
both hands open as shuto)

47.
Morote Kaishu-Gamae

(move right toes and left toes
back at same time,
both hands open as shuto)

48.
Morote Kaishu-Gamae

(move right heel and left heel back at same time)

53.
Naore

49.
Morote Kaishu-Gamae

(move right toes and left toes back at same time)

50.
(step back right foot, heel together, stand straight. left shuto at side of right fist)

51.
(both hands down, right hand over left hand)

52.
(hands at side)

心波二段

Shinpa-Nidan

33

Chapter Five
Shinpa Nidan

Alternate names: Shimpa-2, Shinpa-2

Meaning of kata name: wave of mind or wave from heart

From whom the author learned kata: Richard 'Biggie' Kim

Lineage and history of kata: Naha-Te (Uechi-Ryu)

Shinpa Nidan was also created by Kenwa Mabuni in the early 40's as Jyuroku. He learned Simpa-1 and Simpa-2 from Kanbun Uechi (1877-1948) when he was in Osaka Japan (1910-1948). The two Shinpa Kata are pieces of Uechi's version of Supa-rinpei (108 steps), which Uechi did not completely learn when he was in Fikien, China under a Chinese Tiger-Fist master named Shushiwa.

1.
Yoi

6.
Migi Sanchin-Dachi
Migite-Mae Kakete-Uke

(step forward with right foot, move slowly with dynamic tension)

2.
Kamae

(left hand over right hand, and heels together)

7.
Migi Sanchin-Dachi
Hidari Hira-Ken Zuki

3.
Hajime
Sanchin-Dachi

(heels and fists open at the same time)

8.
Hidari Sanchin-Dachi
Hidarite-Mae Kakete-Uke

(step forward with left foot, move slowly with dynamic tension)

4.
Hidari Sanchin-Dachi
Hidarite-Mae Kakete-Uke

(step forward with left foot, move slowly with dynamic tension)

9.
Hidari Sanchin-Dachi
Migi Hira-Ken Zuki

5.
Hidari Sanchin-Dachi
Migi Hira-Ken Zuki

10.
Hidari Sanchin-Dachi
Migi Hira-Ken Zuki

11.
Hidari Sanchin-Dachi
Migi Hira-Ken Zuki

12a.
Migi Mae Geri

(chamber)

12b.
Migi Mae Geri

(snap kick)

12c.
Migi Mae Geri

(chamber)

13.
Hidari Sanchin-Dachi
Hidarite-Mae Kakete-Uke

(put right foot down then step in
with left foot, move slowly
w/ dynamic tension)

14.
Migi Hiji-Ate

(step forward with right foot)

15.
(move right foot cross over left
foot)

16.
Hidari Sanchin-Dachi
Hidarite-Mae Kakete-Uke

(turn around counter clockwise
then move slowly with dynamic
tension)

17.
Hidari Sanchin-Dachi
Migi Hira-Ken Zuki

18.
Migi Sanchin-Dachi
Migite-Mae Kakete-Uke

(step forward with left foot,
move slowly w/ dynamic tension)

19.
Hidari Sanchin-Dachi
Migi Hira-Ken Zuki

24a.
Migi Mae Geri

(chamber)

20.
Hidari Sanchin-Dachi
Hidarite-Mae Kakete-Uke

(step forward with left foot, move
slowly with dynamic tension)

24b.
Migi Mae Geri

(snap kick)

21.
Hidari Sanchin-Dachi
Migi Hira-Ken Zuki

24c.
Migi Mae Geri

(chamber)

22.
Hidari Sanchin-Dachi
Hidari Hira-Ken Zuki

25.
Migi Kasei-Zenkutsu-Dachi
Hidari Gedan,
Migi Jodan-Uke

(put the right foot down, look to
left, and step with left foot out)

23.
Hidari Sanchin-Dachi
Migi Hira-Ken Zuki

26.
Migi Zenkutsu-Dachi
Migi Ura-Ken
Hidari Soe-Te

(step forward with right foot)

27.
(half step forward with left foot)

28.
Migi Zenkutsu-Dachi
Migi Hiji-Ate
Hidari Soe-Te-Uke

(half step forward with right foot)

29.
(move right foot cross over left foot)

30.
Hidari Sanchin-Dachi
Hidarite-Mae Kakete-Uke

(turn around counter clockwise fast, then move slowly with dynamic tension)

31.
Hidari Sanchin-Dachi
Migi Hira-Ken Zuki

32.
Migi Sanchin-Dachi
Migite-Mae Kakete-Uke

(step forward with left foot, move slowly with dynamic tension)

33.
Hidari Sanchin-Dachi
Hidari Hira-Ken Zuki

34.
Hidari Sanchin-Dachi
Hidarite-Mae Kakete-Uke

(step forward with left foot, move slowly with dynamic tension)

35.
Hidari Sanchin-Dachi
Migi Hira-Ken Zuki

36.
Hidari Sanchin-Dachi
Hidari Hira-Ken Zuki

37.
Hidari Sanchin-Dachi
Migi Hira-Ken Zuki

42.
Migi Shiko-Dachi
Morote-Koken-Uke

(dynamic tension)

38a.
Migi Mae Geri

(chamber)

43.
Hidari Shiko-Dachi
Morote-Koken-Uke

(step back with right foot, move slowly w/ dynamic tension)

38b.
Migi Mae Geri

(snap kick)

44.
Migi Shiko-Dachi
Morote-Koken-Uke

(step back with left foot, move slowly w/ dynamic tension)

38c.
Migi Chudan-Mae Geri

(chamber)

45.
Yame

39.
(put the right foot down, and step left foot forward then turn around clockwise)

46.
Naore

新垣十三歩

ARAKAKI-SEISAN

Chapter Six
Arakaki Seisan

Alternate name: Seishan

Meaning of kata name: thirteen. Usually interpreted as, "Thirteen modes of attack and defense" or "13 positions to attack/defend from".

From whom the author learned kata: Richard 'Biggie' Kim

Lineage and history of kata: Naha-Te (Goju-Ryu)

Arakaki Seisan combines the "Three Challenges" concept, usually interpreted as three Modes/Conflicts: Mind, Body and Spirit. An alternate interpretation of "Three Challenges" is softness, timing, and power. Students can go back and further develop those elements in the previous forms.

1.
Yoi

6.
Hidari Sanchin-Dachi
Migi Chudan Uchi-Uke

2.
Kamae
(left hand over right hand, and heels together)

7.
Migi Sanchin-Dachi
Migi Chudan Uchi-Uke

(keep the right inside block, step forward with right foot, move slowly with dynamic tension)

3.
Hajime
Sanchin-Dachi

(heels and fists open at the same time)

8.
Migi Sanchin-Dachi
Hidari Chudan Gyaku-Zuki

4.
Hidari Sanchin-Dachi
Hidarite-Mae Chudan-Uke

(step forward with left foot, move slowly w/ dynamic tension)

9.
Hidari Sanchin-Dachi
Migi Chudan Uchi-Uke

5.
Hidari Sanchin-Dachi
Migi Chudan Gyaku-Zuki

10.
Hidari Sanchin-Dachi

(keep the left inside block, step in with right foot, move slowly w/ dynamic tension)

44

11.
Hidari Sanchin-Dachi
Migi Chudan Gyaku
Ippon-Ken Zuki

16.
Migi Sanchin Dachi
Migi Kakete-Uke
Hidari Shotei-Uke

(step forward with right foot)

12.
Hidari Sanchin-Dachi
Hidari Chudan Gyaku
Ippon-Ken Zuki

16a.
(front view)

13.
Hidari Sanchin-Dachi
Ryo-Hiji Yoko

17.
Migi Sanchin-Dachi
Migi Jodan-Nuki-Te
Hidari Shotei-Uke

14.
Hidari Sanchin-Dachi
Ryo-Te Jodan Uke

17a.
(front view)

15.
Hidari Sanchin-Dachi
Morote Gedan Shotei-Uke

(move right foot behind left foot,
and turn around clockwise 180'
degree)

18.
Hidari Sanchin Dachi
Hidari Kakete-Uke
Migi Shotei-Uke

(step forward with left foot,
move slowly w/ dynamic
tension)

19.
Hidari Sanchin Dachi
Hidari Jodan-Nukite
Migi Shotei-Uke

24.
Hidari Zenkutsu-Dachi
Migi Oi-Zuki

20.
Migi Sanchin Dachi
Migi Kakete-Uke
Hidari Shotei-Uke

(step forward with right foot)

25a.
Migi Mae-Geri

(chamber)

21.
Migi Sanchin-Dachi
Migi Jodan-Nuki-Te
Hidari Shotei-Uke

25b.
Migi Mae-Geri

(snap kick)

22.
Hidari Zenkutsu-Dachi
Hidari Uchi-Uke

(look to left, and step forward with left foot)

25c.
Migi Mae-Geri

(chamber)

23.
Hidari Zenkutsu-Dachi
Migi Gyaku-Zuki

26.
Hidari Zenkutsu-Dachi
Migi Gyaku-Zuki

(bring right foot back)

27.
Migi Zenkutsu-Dachi
Migi Uchi-Uke

(turn around clockwise)

30c.
Hidari Mae-Geri

(chamber)

28.
Migi Zenkutsu-Dachi
Hidari Gyaku-Zuki

31.
Migi Zenkutsu-Dachi
Hidari Gyaku-Zuki

(bring left foot back)

29.
Migi Zenkutsu-Dachi
Migi Oi-Zuki

32.
Hidari Zenkutsu-Dachi
Hidari Uchi-Uke

(look to left, step forward with left foot)

30a.
Hidari Mae-Geri

(chamber)

33.
Hidari Zenkutsu-Dachi
Migi Gyaku-Zuki

30b.
Hidari Mae-Geri

(snap kick)

34.
Hidari Zenkutsu-Dachi
Hidari Oi-Zuki

35a.
Migi Mae-Geri

(chamber)

38.
Migi Hiji-Otoshi

(right fist over head and
drop right elbow down,
stand heel together)

35b.
Migi Mae-Geri

(snap kick)

39.
Migi Ura-Ken

35c.
Migi Mae-Geri

(chamber)

40.
Migi Uchi-Uke

36.
Hidari Zenkutsu-Dachi
Migi Gyaku-Zuki

41.
(step forward with left foot
crossong over right foot,
keep inside block)

37.
(look back clockwise, move right
foot to left foot and right fist up)

42a.
Migi Mae-Geri

(chamber)

42b.
Migi Mae-Geri

(snap kick)

46.
(look back counter clockwise, move left foot to right foot and left fist up)

42c.
(bring knee back and right fist ready for down block)

47.
Hidari Hiji-Otoshi

(right fist over head and drop right elbow down, stand heel together)

43.
Migi Zenkutsu-Dachi
Migi Gedan-Barai

48.
Hidari Ura-Ken

44.
Migi Zenkutsu-Dachi
Hidari Gyaku-Zuki

49.
Hidari Uchi-Uke

45.
Migi Zenkutsu-Dachi
Migi Jodan Age-Uke

50.
(step in with right foot crossong over left foot, keep left inside block)

51a.
Hidari Mae-Geri

(chamber)

54.
Hidari Zenkutsu-Dachi
Hidari Jodan Age-Uke

51b.
Hidari Mae-Geri

(snap kick)

55.
(same as 37)

51c.
(bring knee back and left fist ready for down block)

56.
Migi Ura-Ken

(same as 38)

52.
Hidari Zenkustu-Dachi
Hidari Gedan-Barai

57.
(same as 41)

53.
Left Front Stance
Right Reverse Punch

Hidari Zenkutsu-Dachi
Migi Gyaku-Zuki

58a.
Right Front Kick

(same as 42)

58b.
Migi Mae-Geri

(snap kick)

62.
Migi Mikazuki-Geri

58c.
(same as 42c)

63. (Kiai)
Hidari Zenkutsu-Dachi
Migi Gyaku-Zuki

(bring right foot back)

59.
Migi Zenkutsu-Dachi
Migi Gedan-Barai

(step forward with right foot)

64.
Hidari Neko-Ashi-Dachi
Morote Jodan Kosa-Uke

(left foot slides back)

60.
Migi Zenkutsu-Dachi
Hidari Gyaku-Zuki

65.
Hidari Neko-Ashi-Dachi

(both hand open to side)

61.
Hidari Kokutsu-Dachi
Hidari Shuto-Uke

(step back with right foot)

66.
Hidari Neko-Ashi-Dachi

(both hand move down slowly,
and right shuto on left palm)

67.
Hidari Neko-Ashi-Dachi
Morote Shotei-Uke

(both hand move clockwise,
left hand high and right hand low,
palm-heels together,)

68.
Hidari Neko-Ashi-Dachi
Morote Shotei-Uke-Gaeshi

(move both hands counter clockwise,
right hand top and left hand down)

69.
Yame

70.
Naore

三十六歩

Sansei Ryu

Chapter Seven
Sanseiryu

Alternate name: Sanseiru

Meaning of kata name: thirty six. Usually interpreted as "thirty-six modes of attack and defense" or "36 positions to attack/defend from."

From whom the author learned kata: Richard Lee

Lineage and history of kata: Naha-Te (Goju-Ryu)

Sanchin (3), Seisan (13), Sanseiryu (36) and Supa-rinpei (108) are typical Southern Chinese style martial arts forms, and there were many different forms with the same name in Southern China. In Okinawa, Southern Chinese style martial arts became popular in early 1800, right before the Opium War, because of Chinese resistance against the UK.

Kanryo Higaonna (1853-1916) would visit Southern China often because, when he was young, he helped his father with his business. His family had a transportation business that carried goods between Okinawa and China. Because of this business he could help bureaucratic officers, who are against Okinawa becoming a part of Japan, escape from Okinawa.

Originally, Higaonna's Sanchin was taught with open hands and natural light breathing, as Sanchin-kata still is in Uechi-ryu. Later it was also revised with closed fists and heavy dynamic breathing by Juhatsu Kyoda, founder of To'on-Ryu, and adopted by Chojun Miyagi as well. According to Higaonna, the purpose of heavy dynamic breathing is nothing but showing off to audience.

1.
Yoi

6.
Hidari Sanchin-Dachi
Migi Chudan Uchi-Uke

2.
Kamae
(left hand over right hand, and
heels together)

7.
Migi Sanchin-Dachi
Migi Chudan Uchi-Uke

(keep the right inside block,
step forward with right foot,
move slowly with dynamic
tension)

3.
Hajime
Sanchin-Dachi

(heels and arms open at the same
time)

8.
Migi Sanchin-Dachi
Hidari Chudan Gyaku-Zuki

4.
Hidari Sanchin-Dachi
Hidarite-Mae Chudan-Uke

(step forward with left foot, move
slowly w/ dynamic tension)

9.
Hidari Sanchin-Dachi
Migi Chudan Uchi-Uke

5.
Hidari Sanchin-Dachi
Migi Chudan Gyaku-Zuki

10.
Hidari Sanchin-Dachi

(keep the left inside block,
step in with right foot, move
slowly w/ dynamic tension)

11.
Hidari Sanchin-Dachi
Migi Gyaku-Zuki

15b.
Migi Sanchin-Dachi
Hidari Shuto Uchi

12.
Hidari Sanchin-Dachi
Migi Chudan Uchi-Uke

16a.
Yoko Geri
(chamber)

13.
Migi Sanchin-Dachi
Migi Chudan Uchi-Uke

(keep the right inside block,
step forward with right foot,
move slowly with dynamic
tension)

16b.
Yoko Geri
(side snap kick)

14.
Migi Sanchin-Dachi
Hidari Gyaku-Zuki

16c.
Yoko Geri
(chamber)

15a.
Migi Sanchin-Dachi
Hidari Shuto Nagashi-Uke

(left shuto chamber)

17.
Ryote Koshi
Musubi-Dachi

(fists are at side, heels together)

18a.
Migi Mae-Geri
(chamber)

21.
Migi Sanchin-Dachi
Migi Higi-Uchi

18b.
Migi Mae-Geri
(front snap kick)

22a.
Migi Yoko-Geri
(chamber)

18c.
Migi Mae-Geri
(chamber)

22b.
Migi Yoko-Geri
(side snap kick)

19.
Migi Sanchin-Dachi
Morote Kakete-Uke

(step forward with right foot)

22c.
Migi Yoko-Geri
(chamber)

20.
Migi Sanchin-Dachi
Hidari Gyaku-Zuki

23.
Hidari Sanchin-Dachi
Hidari Chudan Uchi-Uke

(look to left, and bring right
foot back)

24a.
Migi Mae-Geri
(chamber)

27.
Migi Sanchin-Dachi
Migi Higi-Uchi

24b.
Migi Mae-Geri
(front snap kick)

28a.
Migi Yoko-Geri
(chamber)

24c.
Migi Mae-Geri
(chamber)

28b.
Migi Yoko-Geri
(side snap kick)

25.
Migi Sanchin-Dachi
Morote Kakete-Uke

(step forward with right foot)

28c.
Migi Yoko-Geri
(chamber)

26.
Migi Sanchin-Dachi
Hidari Gyaku-Zuki

29.
Hidari Sanchin-Dachi
Hidari Chudan Uchi-Uke

(look to left, and bring right
foot back)

30a.
Migi Mae-Geri

(chamber)

33.
Migi Sanchin-Dachi
Migi Higi-Uchi

30b.
Migi Mae-Geri

(front snap kick)

34a.
Migi Yoko-Geri
(chamber)

30c.
Migi Mae-Geri

(chamber)

34b.
Migi Yoko-Geri
(side snap kick)

31.
Migi Sanchin-Dachi
Morote Kakete-Uke

(step forward with right foot)

34c.
Migi Yoko-Geri
(chamber)

32.
Migi Sanchin-Dachi
Hidari Gyaku-Zuki

35.
Hidari Sanchin-Dachi
Hidari Chudan Uchi-Uke

(look to left, and turn back
counter clockwise 180 degrees,
bring right foot back)

36.
Migi Sanchin-Dachi
Migi Chudan Uchi-Uke

41a.
Migi Mae-Geri
(chamber)

37.
Shiko-Dachi
Morote Jyodan-Uke

(look to left, step forward with right foot)

41b.
Migi Mae-Geri
(front snap kick)

38.
Shiko-Dachi
Morote Shuto Jodan-Uke

(look to back, step forward with left foot)

41c.
Migi Mae-Geri
(chamber)

39.
Migi Kokutsu-Dachi
Migi Shuto Jodan-Uke
Hidari Haito Gedan-Uke

(look to left 45 degrees, and step forward with right foot)

42.
Migi Kokutsu-Dachi
Morote Yama-Zuki

(step in with right foot)

40.
Migi Kokutsu-Dachi
Morote *Tora-Guchi

(*Tora-Guchi is Mawashi-Uke in Goju)

43.
Hidari Kokutsu-Dachi
Hidari Shuto Jodan-Uke
Migi Haito Gedan-Uke

(look to left, and turn back counter clockwise 180 degrees)

61

44.
Hidari Kokutsu-Dachi
Morote *Tora-Guchi

47.
Musubi-Dachi

(fists are at side, step in with right foot, heels together)

45a.
Hidari Mae-Geri
(chamber)

48.
Hidari Zenkutsu-Dachi
Morote Shuto Jodan-Uke

(step in with left foot)

45b.
Hidari Mae-Geri
(front snap kick)

49.
Migi Shiko-Dachi
Morote Koken-Uke

(look to right, and turn back clockwise)

45c.
Hidari Mae-Geri
(chamber)

50.
Yame

46.
Hidari Kokutsu-Dachi
Morote Yama-Zuki

(step in with left foot)

51.
Naore

久留頓破

KURURUNHA

Chapter Eight
Kururunha

Alternate name: Kururunfa

Meaning of kata name: "to detain long enough to suddenly rip apart" but the real Chinese translation is still unknown.

From whom the author learned kata: Richard Lee

Lineage and history of kata: Naha-Te (Goju-Ryu)

The original Kururunfa may not be as old as most Okinawan practitioners claim. Possibly Chojun Miyagi (1885-1953) brought back Kururunfa and Se-pai kata from China to Okinawa in 1915. This kata, like the Seisan, epitomizes Goju-concepts that combine fast and slow, hard and soft movements.

1.
Yoi

5b.
Migi Gedan Yoko-Geri

(snap lower side kick)

2.
Kamae
(left hand over right hand, and heels together)

5c.
Migi Yoko-Geri
Ryoken Mae

(chamber, fists are at front)

3.
Migi Shizen-Dachi
Morote Haito-Uke

(look to right 45 degrees, step in with right foot)

6.
Hidari Shizen-Dachi
Morote Haito-Uke

(put right foot down, look to left 45 degrees, and step in with left foot)

4.
Migi Kokutsu-Dachi
Migi Chudan Shuto-Uke

(step forward with right foot)

7.
Hidari Kokutsu-Dachi
Hidari Chudan Shuto-Uke

(step forward with left foot)

5a.
Migi Yoko-Geri
Ryoken Mae

(chamber, fists are at front)

8a.
Hidari Yoko-Geri
Ryoken Mae

(chamber, fists are at front)

8b.
Hidari Yoko-Geri
Ryoken Mae

(snap lower side kick)

12.
Migi Sanchin-Dachi
Migi Chudan Shotei-Uke
Hidari Gedan Shotei-Uke

(step forward with right foot, move slowly with dynamic tension)

8c.
Hidari Yoko-Geri
Ryoken Mae

(chamber, fists are at front)

13.
Hidari Sanchin-Dachi
Migi Gedan Shotei-Uke
Hidari Chudan Shotei-Uke

(body shift to left 45 degrees left foot front Sanchin-dachi, but look straight ahead)

9.
Hidari Sanchin-Dachi
Migi Gedan Shotei-Uke
Hidari Chudan Shotei-Uke

(step forward with left foot, move slowly with dynamic tension)

14.
Migi Sanchin-Dachi
Migi Chudan Shotei-Uke
Hidari Gedan Shotei-Uke

(body shift back to front)

10.
Migi Sanchin-Dachi
Migi Gedan Shotei-Uke
Hidari Chudan Shotei-Uke

(body shift to right 45 degrees right foot front Sanchin-dachi, but look straight ahead)

15.
Hidari Sanchin-Dachi
Migi Gedan Shotei-Uke
Hidari Chudan Shotei-Uke

(step forward with left foot, move slowly with dynamic tension)

11.
Hidari Sanchin-Dachi
Migi Gedan Shotei-Uke
Hidari Chudan Shotei-Uke

(body shift back to front)

16.
Migi Sanchin-Dachi
Migi Gedan Shotei-Uke
Hidari Chudan Shotei-Uke

(body shift to right 45 degrees right foot front Sanchin-dachi, but look straight ahead)

17.
Hidari Sanchin-Dachi
Migi Gedan Shotei-Uke
Hidari Chudan Shotei-Uke

(body shift back to front)

21b.
Migi Mae-Geri

(snap front kick)

18.
(look to left 45 degrees)

21c.
Migi Mae-Geri
(chamber)

19.
Hidari Zenkutsu-Dachi
Migi Jodan Nukite

(step in with left foot)

22a.
Hidari Shotei-Uke
Migi-Ken Koshi

20.
Hidari Zenkutsu-Dachi
Migi Chudan Shoutei-Uke
Hidari Shita-Zuki

22b.
Migi Kosa-Dachi
Migi Shita-Zuki

(step in with right foot)

21a.
Migi Mae-Geri
(chamber)

23.
Migi Shiko-Dachi
Migi-Kaishu Koshi
Hidari Chudan Shotei-Uke

(step back with left foot)

24.
Migi Shiko-Dachi
Migi Hiji-Uchi
Hidari Chudan Shotei-Uke

28a.
Hdari Mae-Geri
(chamber)

25.
Migi Zenkutsu-Dachi
Migi Yoko-Hiji-Ate
Hidari-Te Mae

(step in with right foot)

28b.
Hidari Mae-Geri
(front snap kick)

26.
(look to right 45 degrees)

28c.
Hdari Mae-Geri
(chamber)

27a.
Hidari Shotei-Uke
Migi-Ken Koshi

(step in 45 degrees with right foot)

29.
Migi Shotei-Uke
Hidari-Ken Koshi

(put left foot down to front)

27b.
Migi Zenkutsu-Dachi
Migi Shita-Zuki
Hidari Chudan Shotei-Uke

30.
Hidari Kosa-Dachi
Hidari Shita-Zuki

(step in with left foot)

31.
Hidari Shiko-Dachi
Migi Chudan Shotei-Uke
Hidari-Kaishu Koshi

(step back with right foot)

36.
Migi Zenkutsu-Dachi
Morote Shita-Zuki

32.
Hidari Shiko-Dachi
Hidari Hiji-Uchi
Migi Chudan Shotei-Uke

37a.
(look to left, shift to left back
45 degrees, and right hand high
and left hand under)

33.
Migi Zenkutsu-Dachi
Ryote Haishu Heikou Gamae

37b.
Hdari Kokutau-Dachi
Hidari Hai-To
Migi-Ken Koshi

34.
Migi Zenkutsu-Dachi
Jodan Kaishu Juji-Uke

38.
Hdari Kokutau-Dachi
Hidari Kake-Te-Uke
Migi-Ken Koshi

35.
(half step up with left foot)

39.
Migi Shiko-Dachi
Migi Gedan-Barai

(step in with right foot)

40a.
(look to right, shift to right back
45 degrees, and left hand high
and right hand under)

44. (Kiai)
Shiko-Dachi
Morote Gedan-Zuki

40b.
Migi Kokutau-Dachi
Migi Hai-To
Hidari-Ken Koshi

45.
Shiko-Dachi
Ryute-Shuto-Yoi

41.
Migi Kokutau-Dachi
Migi Kake-Te-Uke
Hidari-Ken Koshi

46.
Heiko-Dachi
Ryote Yoko-Shuto-Uchi

42.
Hidari Shiko-Dachi
Hidari Gedan-Barai

(step in with left foot)

47.
Heiko-Dachi
Ryote Yama-Gamae

43.
Hidari Nami-Ashi
Ryoken Koshi

(look to right, turn clockwise to
front, and complete Nami-Ashi)

48.
Heiko-Dachi
Haishu-Awase

49.
Heiko-Dachi
Ryoken Awase

(fists are behind head)

54.
Migi Kokutsu-Dachi
Morote Shuto-Osae

(step in with right foot to right 45 degrees)

50. (Kiai)
Shiko-Dachi
Ryote-Shotei-Osae

55.
Hidari Kokutsu-Dachi
Morote Shuto-Osae

(step in with left foot to left 45 degrees)

51.
Migi Zenkutsu-Dachi
Ryote Jodan Osae

56.
Hidari Kiba-Dachi

(step in with right foot and look to left)

52.
Musubi-Dachi
Ryo-Ken Mae

(step in with left foot and turn counter clockwise to 180 degrees)

57.
Hidari Kiba-Dachi
Hidari Haishu-Uke

53. (Kiai)
View from behind

58.
Migi Mikazuki-Geri

59.
(turn counter clockwise, and put right foot back)

64.
Migi Nami-Ashi

60.
Hidari Neko-Ashi-Dachi
Migi Yoko-Shuto
Hidari Hai-Shu Osae

65.
Migi Neko-Ashi-Dachi

61.
Hidari Neko-Ashi-Dachi
Ryo-Te Kake-Te-Uke

66.
Hidari Kosa-Dachi
Ryo-Te Osae

(step forward with left foot)

62.
Hidari Nami-Ashi

67.
Migi Yoko Keage
Migi Hai-To

(side snap kick)

63.
Hidari Neko-Ashi-Dachi

68.
(step forward with right foot)

69.
Migi Kosa-Dachi
Shuto Juji-Uke

(step in with right foot)

72c. (Kiai)
Musubi-Dachi
Mawashi-Uke

70.
Migi Kiba-Dachi
Migi Haishu-Uke

(step out with left foot)

73.
Yame

71.
Migi Kakato Neko-Dachi
Migi Shotei-Uchi Uke
Mawashi-Uke Yoi

(slide back right foot with toes up)

74.
Naore

72a.
Musubi-Dachi
Mawashi-Uke

72b.
Musubi-Dachi
Mawashi-Uke

新垣 二十四歩

Arakaki Niseishi

Chapter Nine
Arakaki Niseishi

Alternate name: Aragaki Niseshi

Meaning of kata name: twenty four steps

From whom the author learned kata: Richard 'Biggie' Kim

Lineage and history of kata: Naha-Te (Goju-Ryu)

Naha-Te (Kume-mura, To-De) kata by Seisho Arakaki (1840-1920). Arakaki served as a Chinese interpreter, and travelled to Beijing in September 1870. His only recorded martial arts instructor from this period was Wan-Shinzan (Wai Xinxian in Chinese) from Fuzhou, a city in the Fujian province of Qing Dynasty China. Arakaki was called Maya-Arakaki, meaning that he can move like cat. He was a famous martial artist because of this uncanny ability. He learned katas such as Unsu (Unshu), Seisan, Sochin, Niseishi and Sanchin (which were later incorporated into different styles of karate), and weapons kata Arakaki-no-kun, Arakaki-no-sai, etc. from Wai Xinxian and Yabu-Pechin.

His students included Kanryo Higaonna (1853–1916, Naha-Te), Gichin Funakoshi (1868–1957; founder of Shotokan), Kanbun Uechi (1877–1948; founder of Uechi-Ryu), Kanken Toyama (1888–1966; founder of Shudokan), Kenwa Mabuni (1889–1952; founder of Shito-Ryu), and Tsuyoshi Chitose (1898–1984; founder of Chito-Ryu).

1.
Yoi

6.
Migi Sanchin-Dachi
RyoKen-Zuki

2.
Kamae

7.
Sanchin-Dachi
Sanchin-Gamae

(step in with left foot)

3.
Hajime

(cross arms, left hand over right
and knees bend)

8.
Migi Sanchin-Dachi
RyoKen-Koshi

(step out with right foot and
fists at side)

4.
Sanchin-Dachi
Sanchin-Gamae

(open both heels out, and
both fists at front)

9.
Migi Sanchin-Dachi
RyoKen-Zuki

5.
Migi Sanchin-Dachi
RyoKen-Koshi

(step out with right foot and
fists at side)

10.
Sanchin-Dachi
Sanchin-Gamae

(step in with left foot)

11.
Migi Sanchin-Dachi
RyoKen-Koshi

(step out with right foot and fists at side)

16a.
Hidari Kosa-Dachi
Migi Jodan Kaishu-Uke
Hidari Haishu Osae-Uke

12.
Migi Sanchin-Dachi
RyoKen-Zuki

16b.
Hidari Kosa-Dachi
Migi Jodan Shuto-Uchi
Hidari Kaishu-Uke

13.
Migi Sanchin-Dachi
Migi Uchi-Uke

17a.
Migi Chudan Mae-Geri

(chamber)

14.
Migi Sanchin-Dachi
Hidari Chudan-Zuki

17b.
Migi Chudan Mae-geri

(snap front kick)

15.
Migi Sanchin-Dachi
Migi Chudan-Zuki

17c.
Migi Chudan Mae-Geri

(chamber)

18.
Migi Kosa-Dachi
Ryo-Shuto Gedan Kosa-Uke

(step forward with right foot)

22.
Hidari Sanchin-Dachi
Migi Ken Koshi
Hidari Kaishu-Uke

19.
Migi Kiba-Dachi
Migi Hai-to

22a.
(front view)

20.
Hidari Sanchin-Dachi
Ryo-Kaisho Koshi

(look to left, step in with right foot)

23.
Hidari Sanchin-Dachi
Migi Chudan Zuki

21.
Hidari Sanchin-Dachi
Ryo Shotei-Ate

24.
Hidari Sanchin-Dachi
Hidari Chudan Zuki

21a. (Kiai)
(front view)

25.
Hidari Kosa-Dachi
Migi Jodan Shuto-Uchi
Hidari Kaishu-Uke

(step in with left foot)

26a.
Migi Chudan Mae-Geri

(chamber)

29.
look to left

26b.
Migi Chudan Mae-Geri

(front snap kick)

30.
Hidari Kosa-Dachi
Migi Jodan Shuto-Uchi
Hidari Kaishu-Uke

26c.
Migi Chudan Mae-Geri

(chamber)

31a.
Migi Chudan Mae-Geri

(chamber)

27.
Migi Shotei-Osae-Uke

(step in with right foot)

31b.
Migi Chudan Mae-geri

(snap front kick)

28.
Migi Kosa-Dachi
Morote Gedan Shuto-Uke

31c.
Migi Chudan Mae-Geri

(chamber)

32.
Migi Zenkutsu-Dachi
Migi Haishu Nagashi-Uke
Hidari-Ken Koshi

37.
Migii Kiba-Dachi
Migi Haishu-Uke
Hidari Ken Koshi

33.
Migi Zenkutsu-Dachi
Migi Kaishu-Uke
Hidari-Ken Koshi

38.
Migi Shuto Gedan-Uke
Hidari-Ken Koshi

(step in half with right foot)

34.
Migi Zenkutsu-Dachi
Hidari Gyaku Zuki

39a.
Migi Kakato Neko-Dachi
Migi Shotei-Uchi Uke
Mawashi-Uke Yoi

(slide back right foot with toes up)

35.
Migi Zenkutsu-Dachi
Migi Oi-Zuki

39b.
Migi Kakato Neko-Dachi
Mawashi-Uke

36.
Migi Kosa-Dachi
Morote Shuto Gedan
Juji-Uke

(step in with left foot)

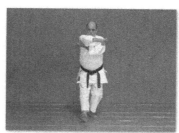

39c
Migi Kakato Neko-Dachi
Mawashi-Uke

40. (Kiai)
Musubi-Dachi
Mawashi-Uke

41.
Yame

42.
Naore

ARAKAKI-UNSU

Chapter Ten
Arakaki Unsu

Alternate name: Aragaki Unsu

Meaning of kata name: cloud hands

From whom the author learned kata: Herbert Lee

Lineage and history of kata: Naha-Te (Kume-mura, To-De)

Arakaki Unsu was originally taught by Seisho Arakaki (1840-1920). Shotokan's Unsu is a longer version, taught by Kenwa Mabuni in the 1940's. Kenwa Mabuni may have added an acrobatic move to the kata to make it longer because the original Okinawan version is quite short.

1.
Yoi

5-b.
Migi Sanchin-Dachi
RyoKen-Gedan

2.
Kamae

6.
Migi Sanchin-Dachi
Migi Uchi-Ike

3.
Hajime

(cross arms, left hand over right
and knees bend)

7.
Migi Sanchin-Dachi
Hidari Chudan-Zuki

4.
Sanchin-Dachi
Sanchin-Gamae

(open both heels out, and
both fists at front)

8.
Migi Sanchin-Dachi
Migi Chudan-Zuki

5-a.
Migi Sanchin-Dachi
RyoKen-Gedan

(step forward with right foot
and cross arms)

9.
Hidari Zenkutsu-Dachi
Hidari Gedan-Barai

(step left with left foot)

88

10.
Hidari Kosa-Dachi
Migi Gyaku-Gedan
Uchi Otoshi

11a.
Migi Mae-Geri
Migi-te Ashi-tori

(chamber)

11b.
Migi Mae-Geri
Migi-te Ashi-tori

(front snap kick)

11c.
Migi Mae-Geri
Migi-te Ashi-tori

(chamber)

12.
Migi Sanchin-Dachi
Migi Kake-te Uke
Hidari Chudan Shotei-Uke

13.
Migi Sanchin-Dachi
Hidari Chdan-Zuki

14.
Migi Sanchin-Dachi
Migi Chudan-Zuki

15.
Migi Sanchin-Dachi
Migi Chudan-Ude-Uke
Hidari-te Osae

16.
(left foot cross over right)

17.
Hidari Sanchin-Dachi
Hidari Chudan Uke

(turn counter clockwise
180 degrees)

18.
Hidari Sanchin-Dachi
Hidari Gedan-Barai

21.
Migi Sanchin-Dachi
Migi Kake-te Uke
Hidari Chudan Shotei-Uke

19.
Hidari Kosa-Dachi
Migi Gyaku-Gedan
Uchi Otoshi

22.
Migi Sanchin-Dachi
Hidari Chdan-Zuki

20a.
Migi Mae-Geri
Migi-te Ashi-tori

(chamber)

23.
Migi Sanchin-Dachi
Migi Chudan-Zuki

20b.
Migi Mae-Geri
Migi-te Ashi-tori

(front snap kick)

24.
Migi Zenkutsu-Dachi
Migi Gedan-Barai

(step left)

20c.
Migi Mae-Geri
Migi-te Ashi-tori

(chamber)

25a.
Hidari Kosa-Dachi
Migi Chudan Shoti-Uke
Hidari Gedan Haito-Uke

25b.
Hidari Kosa-Dachi
Migi Kake-te-Uke

28.
Migi Sashi-Te

26a.
Migi Mae-Geri
Migi Kake-te Uke

(chamber)

29.
Hidari Zenkutsu-Dachi
Hidari Chdan-Oi-Zuki

(step forward w/ left foot)

26b.
Migi Mae-Geri
Migi Kake-te Uke

(front snap kick)

30.
Migi Zenkutsu-Dachi
Migi Chudan-Oi-Zuki

(step back w/ left foot)

26c.
Migi Mae-Geri
Migi Kake-te Uke

(chamber)

31.
Migi Zenkutsu-Dachi
Hidari Chudan-Gyaku
-Zuki

27.
Migi Zenkutsu-Dachi
Hidari Chudan-Gyaku-Zuki

32.
Migi Zenkutsu-Dachi
Migi Chudan-Oi-Zuki

33.
Migi Mikazuki-Geri

37.
Hidari Zenkutsu-Dachi
Hidari Chdan-Oi-Zuki

(step forward w/ left foot)

34.
Ryo-te Fuse-Gamae

38.
Hidari Kosa-Dachi
Migi Gyaku-Gedan
Uchi Otoshi

35.
Ryo-te Fuse-Gamae

(look to right 45 degrees)

39.
Hidari Kosa-Dachi
Migi Jodan-Uchi-Uke

36a.
(stand up and half step in with left foot)

40.
Hidari Kosa-Dachi
Migi Jodan-Uchi-Uke
Hidari-te Jyodan-Osae

36b.
Migi Koukutsu-Dachi
Migi Chudan-Shuto-Uke

41.
Hidari Kosa-Dachi
Migi Jodan-Uchi-Uke
Hidari-te Chudan-Osae

92

42a.
Hidari Kosa-Dachi

(cross arms)

45.
Hidari Shiko-Dachi
Migi Sashi-te

(right foot back)

43b.
Hidari Kosa-Dachi
Ryo-te Gedan-Gamae

46.
Hidari Shiko-Dachi
Hidari Chudan-Zuki

44a.
Migi Mae-Geri
Ryo-te Gedan-Gamae

(chamber)

47.
Hidari Zenkutsu-Dachi
Hidari Gedan-Uke

(step left 90 degrees)

44b.
Migi Mae-Geri
Ryo-te Gedan-Gamae

(front snap kick)

48a.
Hidari Kosa-Dachi
Migi Gyaku-Gedan
Uchi Otoshi

44c.
Migi Mae-Geri
Ryo-te Gedan-Gamae

(chamber)

48b.
Hidari Kosa-Dachi
Migi Gyaku-Gedan
Uchi Otoshi

49.
Hidari Kosa-Dachi
Migi Jodan-Uchi-Uke

53a.
Migi Mae-Geri
Ryo-te Gedan-Gamae

(chamber)

50.
Hidari Kosa-Dachi
Migi Jodan-Uchi-Uke
Hidari-te Jyodan-Osae

53b.
Migi Mae-Geri
Ryo-te Gedan-Gamae

(front snap kick)

51.
Hidari Kosa-Dachi
Migi Jodan-Uchi-Uke
Hidari-te Chudan-Osae

53c.
Migi Mae-Geri
Ryo-te Gedan-Gamae

(chamber)

52a.
Hidari Kosa-Dachi

(cross arms)

54a.
Hidari Shiko-Dachi
Migi Sashi-te

(right foot back)

52b.
Hidari Kosa-Dachi
Ryo-te Gedan-Gamae

54b.
Hidari Shiko-Dachi
Hidari Chudan-Zuki

94

55a.
Migi Neko-Ashi-Dachi
Hidari Haito-Uke Yoi
Migi Soe-te

57.
Yame

55b.
Migi Neko-Ashi-Dachi
Hidari Haito-Uchi-Uke
Migi Soe-te

58.
Naore

56a.
Migi Neko-Ashi-Dachi
Mawashi-Uke

56b.
Migi Neko-Ashi-Dachi
Mawashi-Uke

56c.
Migi Neko-Ashi-Dachi
Morote Shoutei-Uke

新垣　壮鎮

ARAKAKI-SOCHIN

Chapter Eleven
Arakaki Sochin

Alternate name: Aragaki Sochin

Meaning of kata name: immovable, rooted to ground

From whom the author learned kata: Richard Lee

Lineage and history of kata: Naha-Te (Kume-mura, To-De)

Arakaki Sochin was originally taught by Seisho Arakaki (1840-1920). This is the original Arakaki version. It is not Shotokan's Sochin as taught by Gigou Funakoshi, Gichin Funakoshi's 3rd son, who had studied under Okinawan Karate master Kori Hisataka (Kudaka for Okinawan, 1907-1988), founder of Shorinji-Ryu Kenkokan Karate.

1.
Yoi

5-b.
Shiko-Dachi
RyoKen-Gedan

2.
Kamae

6.
Migi Sanchin-Dachi
Sanchin-Gamae

(step forward with right foot, both fists at front)

3.
Hajime

(drop body, bend knees outward and both fists at front)

7.
Migi Sanchin-Dachi
Hidari Hiki-te

(left fist chamber)

4.

(open both heels out, cross arms left hand over right)

8.
Migi Sanchin-Dachi
Hidarii Chudan-Zuki

5-a.
Shiko-Dachi

(both toes out, arms move down slowly)

9.
Migi Sanchin-Dachi
Sanchin-Gamae

10.
Hidargi Sanchin-Dachi
Sanchin-Gamae

(step forward with left foot and both fists at front)

15.
Migi Sanchin-Dachi
Hidari Hiki-te

(left fist chamber)

11.
Hidari Sanchin-Dachi
Migi Hiki-te

(right fist chamber)

16.
Migi Sanchin-Dachi
Hidarii Chudan-Zuki

12.
Hidarii Sanchin-Dachi
Migi Chudan-Zuki

17.
Migi Sanchin-Dachi
Sanchin-Gamae

13.
Hidargi Sanchin-Dachi
Sanchin-Gamae

18.
Migi Kosa-Dachi

(right foot step cross over left foot, left fist under right elbow)

14.
Migi Sanchin-Dachi
Sanchin-Gamae

(step forward with right foot and both fists at front)

19.
Hidari Sanchin-Dachi
Sanchin-Gamae

(turn around counter clockwise 180 degrees to face rear)

20.
Hidari Sanchin-Dachi
Migi Hiki-te

(right fist chamber)

25.
Migi Sanchin-Dachi
Hidarii Chudan-Zuki

21.
Hidarii Sanchin-Dachi
Migi Chudan-Zuki

26.
Migi Sanchin-Dachi
Sanchin-Gamae

22.
Hidargi Sanchin-Dachi
Sanchin-Gamae

27.
Hidargi Sanchin-Dachi
Sanchin-Gamae

(step forward with left foot, both fists at front)

23.
Migi Sanchin-Dachi
Sanchin-Gamae

(step forward with right foot, both fists at front)

28.
Hidari Sanchin-Dachi
Migi Hiki-te

(right fist chamber)

24.
Migi Sanchin-Dachi
Hidari Hiki-te

(left fist chamber)

29.
Hidarii Sanchin-Dachi
Migi Chudan-Zuki

30.
Hidargi Sanchin-Dachi
Sanchin-Gamae

35.
Hidari Kokutsu-Dachi
Hidari Shuto-Uke

31. Kiai
Yoko-Shizen-Tai
Migi Tettsui-Uchi

36.
Migi Kokutsu-Dachi
Migi Shuto-Uke

32.
Hidargi Kokutsu-Dachi
Migi-Chudan,
Hidari-Gedan-Uke

37.
Hidari Zenkutsu-Dachi
Ryoken Hiki-te

(both fists chamber)

33.
Hidargi Kokutsu-Dachi
Migi-Gedan-Zuki,
Hidari-Hiki-Uke

38. (Kiai)
Hidari Zenkutsu-Dachi
Ryoken Chudan-Zuki

34.
Migi Kokutsu-Dachi
Migi Shuto-Uke

39.
Hidari Zenkutsu-Dachi
Ryote Joudan-Uke

40.
Hidargi Zenkutsu-Dachi
Migi Gedan Mawashi
-Tettsui-Awase-Uchi

44b.
Migi Chudan-Geri

(right snap kick)

41.

(half step forward with right foot)

44c.
Migi Chudan-Geri

(chamber)

42.
Hidargi Zenkutsu-Dachi
Ryoken-Chudan-Gamae

45.
Hidargi Kokutsu-Dachi
Migi-Chudan,
Hidari-Gedan-Uke

43.
Hidargi Kosa-Dachi
Migi Jodan Shuto-Uchi,
Hidari-Hiki-te-Uke

46.
Hidargi Kokutsu-Dachi
Migi-Gedan-Zuki,
Hidari-Hiki-Uke

44a.
Migi Chudan-Geri

(chamber)

47.
Migi Zenkutsu-Dachi
Migi Jodan-Tate-Shuto
-Uke

104

48.
Migi Zenkutsu-Dachi
Hidari Gyaku-Zuki

52-a. (side view)

49.
Migi Zenkutsu-Dachi
Hidari Shuto-Nagashi
-Uchi-Uke

53.
Migi Zenkutsu-Dachi
Hidari Shuto-Osae-Uke,
Migi Ushiro-Shuto

(left foot step back slowly)

50.
Migi Zenkutsu-Dachi
Hidari Tate-Shuto-Uke

54.
Hidari Zenkutsu-Dachi
Migi Shuto-Osae-Uke,
Hidari Ushiro-Shuto

(right foot step back slowly)

51. (Kiai)
Migi Zenkutsu-Dachi
Migi Tate-Hiji-Uchi

55.
Hidari Zenkutsu-Dachi
Ryote Jodan-Juji-Uke

52.
Hidari Zenkutsu-Dachi
Migi Shuto-Osae-Uke,
Hidari Ushiro-Shuto

(right foot step back slowly)

56.
Hidari Zenkutsu-Dachi

(hands open to side)

57a.
Migi Chudan-Mae-Geri

(Chamber)

60.
Hidari Zenkutsu-Dachi
Hidari Chudan-Zuki

57b.
Migi Chudan-Mae-Geri
Ryo-te Hasami-Uke

61.
Musubi-Dachi
Hidari Shuto-Osae-Uke,
Migi Shuto-Awase

(left foot back to right foot)

57c.
Migi Chudan-Mae-Geri
Ryo-te Hasami-Uke

(chamber)

62a.
Musubi-Dachi
Ryo-te Gedan-Juji-Gaeshi

58.
Hidari Zenkutsu-Dachi
Hidari Jodan Shotei-Osae

62b.
Musubi-Dachi
Ryo-te Gedan-Juji-Gaeshi

59.
Hidari Zenkutsu-Dachi
Migi Chudan-Gyaku-Zuki

63.
Yame

64. Naore

106

糸州 鷺牌

ITOSU-LOHAI

Chapter Twelve
Itosu Lohai

Alternate names: Itosu Rohai, Itoso Lohai

Meaning of kata name: crane stance

From whom the author learned kata: Lefty Nakayama

Lineage and history of kata: Tomari-Te

Itosu Lohai is one of Anko Itosu's (1831-1915) recreation-kata from an old Tomari-Te version. Itosu is famous for the creation of modern kata and the five Pinans. He also recreated the three Naihanchi (Tekki), Passai Sho (Bassai-Dai), Shiho-Kosokun and the Itosu-Lohai.

1.
Yoi

6.
Kiba-Dachi
Migi Tate-Nukite

2.
Kamae

(left hand over right hand and hells together)

7.
Kiba-Dachi

(left hand under right arm)

3.
Kiba-Dachi
Morote Jodan Haito-Uke

(step side with right foot)

8.
Kiba-Dachi
Hidari Tete-Shuto-Uke

4.
Kiba-Dachi
Migi Jodan-Uke

9.
Kiba-Dachi
Migi Tate-Kagi-Zuki

5.
Kiba-Dachi
Hidari Tettsui

10.
Kiba-Dachi
Morote Jodan Haito-Uke

(right foot step over left foot, turn 180 degrees to face rear)

110

11.
Kiba-Dachi

(left haito and right fist chamber)

15a.

(back view)

12.
Kiba-Dachi
Migi Jodan-Zuki

16.
Kokutsu-Dachi
Hidari Jodan Shuto-Uke
Migi Gedan Shotei-Osae

(step back with right foot)

13.
Kiba-Dachi
Hidari Chudan-Zuki

17.
Kokutsu-Dachi
Hidari Tettsui

14.
Kiba-Dachi
Migi Chudan-Zuki

18.
Migi Zenkutsu-Dachi
Migi Tate-Oi-Zuki

15.
Migi-Mae Sagi-Ashi-Dachi
Hidari Jodan Shuto-Uke
Migi Gedan Shotei-Osae

19.
Migi-Mae Sagi-Ashi-Dachi
Hidari Jodan Shuto-Uke
Migi Gedan Shotei-Osae

20.
Migi Zenkutsu-Dachi
Migi Tate-Oi-Zuki

25.
Musubi-Dachi

(left foot back to right foot,
chamber, right fist over left)

21.
Migi Zenkutsu-Dachi

(chamber, right fist over left)

26.
Migi Zenkutsu-Dachi
Ryu-ken Yama-Zuki

22.
Migi Zenkutsu-Dachi
Ryu-ken Yama-Zuki

27a.

(turn counter clockwisw,
360 degrees)

23.
Musubi-Dachi

(right foot back to left foot,
chamber, left fist over right)

27b.

(continue)

24.
Hidari Zenkutsu-Dachi
Ryo-ken Yama-Zuki

27c.
Right Kokutsu-Dachi
Right Shuto-Uke

28.
Hidari Kokutsu-Dachi
Hidari Shuto-Uke

(step back with right foot)

29. (Kiai)
Kiba-Dachi
Moro-Te Jodan Haito-Uke

30.
Yame

31.
Naore

Matsu-mora Lohai

松茂良 鷺牌

Nobu K
2007

Chapter Thirteen
Matsumora Lohi

Alternate name: Rohai

Meaning of kata name: crane stance

From whom the author learned kata: Richard Lee

Lineage and history of kata: Tomari-Te

Matsumora Lohai was originally taught by Kosaku Matsumora (1829-1896). It was called Matsumora Lohai, or Rohai, after Kosaku Matsumora who was presumably its inventor. Anko Itosu (1831-1915) later took this kata and developed three other kata from it: Rohai-Shodan, Rohai-Nidan, and Rohai-Sandan. In Shorin-Ryu and Matsubayashi-Ryu, this kata introduces Gedan Shotei Ate (Lower/Downward Palm Heel Smash) and Ippon Ashi Dachi (One Leg Stance). It contains a sequence of Tomoe Zuki (Circular Punch) exactly the same as the one in Bassai, though the ending of the sequence changes into Hangetsu Geri/Uke (Half Moon Kick/Block).

In modern Karate, some styles teach all three kata (such as Shito-Ryu). However, other styles employ only one of them as a kata (such as Wado-Ryu, which teaches Rohai-Shodan as Rohai). Gichin Funakoshi, founder of Shotokan, redeveloped and renamed Rohai as Meikyo, which means literally "bright mirror", often translated as "mirror of the soul." Meikyo is a combination of all three different Rohai Kata, containing elements of each.

1.
Yoi

5b.
Kiba-Dachi
Morote Gedan Shuto-Uke

(step side with right foot)

2.
Kamae

(left hand over right hand and heels together)

6a.
Kiba-Dachi

(left hand under right arm)

3.
Shizen-Dachi
Morote Gedan Haito-Uke

(step side with right foot)

6b.
Kiba-Dachi
Hidari Tete-Shuto-Uke

4.
Shizen-Dachi
Migi Jodan Haito-Uke
Hidari Shuto Soe-te

7.
Kiba-Dachi
Migi Kagi-Zuki

5a.
Shizen-Dachi
Morote Gedan-Uke Yoi

8.
Migi Neko Ashi-Dachi
Ryo-Ken Koshi

(half step back with left foot, then step forward with right foot, fists on side)

9.
(step forward with right foot)

14a.
Migi Shizen-Dachi
Migi Haito-Uke Yoi

(step right 45 degrees front with right foot)

10.
(step left 45 degrees forward with left foot)

14b.
Migi Shizen-Dachi
Migi Haito-Uke
Hidari Shuto Soe-te

11.
(step right 45 degrees forward with right foot)

15.
Migi Shizen-Dachi
Migi Chudan Oi-Zuki

12.
(step left 45 degrees forward with left foot)

16.
Migi Shizen-Dachi
Hidari Chudan Gyaku-Zuki

13.
Hidari Ippon Ashi-Dachi
Migi Gedan Shotei-Uke
Hidari Jodan Shuto-Uke

17.
Migi Shizen-Dachi
Migi Chudan Oi-Zuki

18.
Hidari Ippon Ashi-Dachi
Migi Gedan Shotei-Uke
Hidari Jodan Shuto-Uke

(turn left 90 degrees front with left foot)

22.
Migi Shizen-Dachi
Migi Chudan Oi-Zuki

19a.
Migi Shizen-Dachi
Migi Haito-Uke Yoi

(step right 45 degrees front with right foot)

23a.
(step back with right foot)

19b.
Migi Shizen-Dachi
Migi Haito-Uke
Hidari Shuto Soe-te

23b.
Kiba-Dachi
Migi Gedan-Zuki
Hidari Sukui-Uke

20.
Migi Shizen-Dachi
Migi Chudan Oi-Zuki

24.
Hidari Ippon Ashi-Dachi
Migi Gedan Shotei-Uke
Hidari Jodan Shuto-Uke

(step back with left foot)

21.
Migi Shizen-Dachi
Hidari Chudan Gyaku-Zuki

25.
Migi Shizen-Dachi
Migi Haito-Uke
Hidari Shuto Soe-te

(step forward with right foot)

26.
Migi Ippon Ashi-Dachi
Hidari Gedan Shotei-Uke
Migi Jodan Shuto-Uke

31.
Hidari Zenkutsu-Dachi
Yama-Zuki

27.
Hidari Shizen-Dachi
Hidari Haito-Uke
Migi Shuto Soe-te

(step forward with left foot)

32.
Migii Heisoku-Dachi
Ryo-ken Hidari Koshi

(step back with left foot,
fists on left side)

28.
Hidari Ippon Ashi-Dachi
Migi Gedan Shotei-Uke
Hidari Jodan Shuto-Uke

33.
Migi Zenkutsu-Dachi
Yama-Zuki

29.
Migi Shizen-Dachi
Migi Haito-Uke
Hidari Shuto Soe-te

(step forward with right foot)

34.
Hidari Kokutsu-Dachi
Hidari Shuto-Uke

(step back with right foot)

30.
Hidari Heisoku-Dachi
Ryo-ken Migi Koshi

(step back with right foot,
fists on right side)

35.
Migi Mikazuki-Geri

121

36a.
(turn counter clockwise 360 degrees,
 right foot cross over left foot)

39.
Naore

36b.
(continue)

36c.
Migi Kokutsu-Dachi
Migi Shuto-Uke

37.
Hidari Kokutsu-Dachi
Hidari Shuto-Uke

(step back with right foot)

38.
Yame

古流 慈恩

KORYU-JION

Chapter Fourteen
Koryu Jion

Alternate names: Original Jion

Meaning of kata name: mercy

From whom the author learned kata: Richard Lee

Lineage and history of kata: Tomari-Te

Koryu Jion is one of the original versions of Jion, possibly practiced by Bokunin Nakazato (1827-1897). However, some say that the Jion Kata was devised in the Jion temple, where martial arts were famously practiced in Fuken, China. Richard 'Biggie' Kim had 4 or 5 different versions of Jion Kata.

1.
Yoi

5.
(look to left 45 degrees)

2.
Kamae

6.
Migi Neko Ashi-Dachi
Morote Chudan Shuto-Uke

(step forward left 45 degrees
with right foot)

3.
Musubi-Dachi
Migi Chudan Hou-Ken

(hold right fist with left hand)

7a.
Migi Chudan Mae-Geri

(chamber)

4a.
(step back with right foot)

7b.
Migi Chudan Mae-Geri

4b.
Hidari Zenkutsu-Dachi
Migi Gedan-Uke
Hidari Chudan-Uke

7c.
Migi Chudan Mae-Geri

(chamber)

8.
Migi Zenkutsu-Dachi
Migi Jodan Oi-Zuki

(step forward with right foot)

12a.
Hidari Chudan Mae-Geri
(chamber)

9.
Migi Zenkutsu-Dachi
Hidari Chudan Gyaku-Zuki

12b.
Hidari Chudan Mae-Geri

10.
Migi Zenkutsu-Dachi
Migi Chudan Oi-Zuki

12c.
Hidari Chudan Mae-Geri
(chamber)

11a.
(step forward right 45 degrees
 with left foot)

13.
Hidari Zenkutsu-Dachi
Hidari Jodan Oi-Zuki

(step forward with left foot)

11b.
Hidari Neko Ashi-Dachi
Morote Chudan Shuto-Uke

14.
Hidari Zenkutsu-Dachi
Migi Chudan Gyaku-Zuki

15.
Hidari Zenkutsu-Dachi
Hidari Chudan Oi-Zuki

20.
Migi Zenkutsu-Dachi
Migi Jodan-Uke

(step forward with right foot)

16.
Migi Jodan Sashi-Te
Hidari-Ken Koshi

21.
Migi Zenkutsu-Dachi
Hidari Gyaku-Jodan-Uke

17.
Hidari Zenkutsu-Dachi
Hidari Jodan-Uke

(step left with left foot)

22.
Migi Zenkutsu-Dachi
Migi Chudan-Zuki

18.
Hidari Zenkutsu-Dachi
Migi Gyaku-Jodan-Uke

23.
Hidari Zenkutsu-Dachi
Hidari Jodan -Uke

(step forward with left foot)

19.
Hidari Zenkutsu-Dachi
Hidari Chudan-Zuki

24.
Hidari Sashi-Te

25.
Migii Zenkutsu-Dachi
Migi Chudan Oi-Zuki

(step forward with right foot)

28.
Kiba-Dachi
Hidari Jodan Yoko-Uke
Migi-Gedan-Uke

(look right)

26a.
(turn counter clockwise 270 degrees, step side with left foot)

29a.
Kiba-Dachi
Hidari-Ken Koshi

26b.
Kiba-Dachi
Migi Jodan Yoko-Uke
Hidari-Gedan-Uke

29a.
Kiba-Dachi
Hidarii Kagi-Zuki

27a.
Kiba-Dachi
Migi-Ken Koshi

30.
Hidari Zenkutsu-Dachi
Hidari Gedan -Uke

(step back with right foot)

27b.
Kiba-Dachi
Migi Kagi-Zuki

31.
Migi Kiba-Dachi
Migi Shotei-Uchi

(step forward with right foot)

129

32.
Musubi-Dachi
Ryo-ken Koshi

(step back with right foot)

36.
Migi Kosa-Dachi
Ryo-ken Gedan-Uke

(step forward with right foot)

33a.
Musubi-Dachi
Ryo-ken Jodan Uke

37.
Hidari Zenkutsu-Dachi
Ryo-Ken Mune-Mae

33b.
Musubi-Dachi
Ryo-ken Jodan Uke

37a.
front view of 37

34.
Musubi-Dachi
Ryo-ken Gedan Ura-ken

38.
Hidari Zenkutsu-Dachi
Ryo-Ura-Ken Yoko-Uchi

35.
Hidari Ippon Ashi-Dachi
Ryo-ken Koshi

39.
Hidari Zenkutsu-Dachi
Migi-Ken Koshi
Hidari-Te Sukui-Uke

130

40.
Kosa-Dachi
Migi Shita-Zuki

(step forward with right foot)

42.
Hidari Zenkutsu-Dachi
Ryo-ken Jodan-Uke

(step forward with left foot)

40a.
(side view of 40)

43a.
Hidari Zenkutsu-Dachi
Hidari Tettsui Awase

41a.
Hidari Chudan Mae-Geri

(chamber)

43b.
Hidari Zenkutsu-Dachi
Hidari Tettsui Awase

41b.
Hidari Chudan Mae-Geri

43-a.
Side view

41c.
Hidari Chudan Mae-Geri

(chamber)

43-b.
side view

44.
Migi Neko-Ashi-Dachi
Ryo-ken Koshi

(turn clockwise 180 degrees)

48b.
Musubi-Dachi
(swing hands over head)

45.
Migi Zenkutsu-Dachi
Ryo-ken Chudan-Zuki

(step forward with right foot)

48c.
(step right side with right foot)

46.
Musubi-Dachi
Ryo-te Sasi-te

(step back with right foot)

48c.
Kiba-Dachi
Moro-te Gedan-Uke

47.
(bend over)

49.
Hidari Kokutsu-Dachi
Hidari Shuto-Uke

(turn left counter clockwise)

48a.
Musubi-Dachi

(swing hands right side)

50.
Hidari Kokutsu-Dachi
Migi Chudan Gyaku-Zuki

51.
Migi Neko-Ashi-Dachi
Ryo-ken Koshi

(turn clockwise 90 degrees)

56.
Kiba-Dachi
Hidari Jodan-Zuki

52.
(step forward with right foot)

57.
Kiba-Dachi
Migi Chudan-Zuki

53.
(step forward with left foot)

58.
Kiba-Dachi
Hidari Chudan-Zuki

54.
Hidari Ippon Ashi-Dachi
Migi Gedan Shotei-Uke
Hidari Jodan Shuto-Uke

59.
Hidari Tachi-Hiza
Migi Otoshi-Zuki
Hidari-ken Mae

55.
Kiba-Dachi
Migi Tate Shuto-Uke

(step back with right foot)

60a.
(stand up with left foot)

60b.
Hidari Ippon Ashi-Dachi
Migi Gedan Shotei-Uke
Hidari Jodan Shuto-Uke

64.
Heisoku-Dachi
Ryo-ken Migi Koshi

61a.
(step back right 45 degrees
with right foot)

65.
Hidari Zenkutsu-Dachi
Yama-Zuki

61b.
Kiba-Dachi
Migi Tate Shuto-Uke

66.
Heisoku-Dachi
Ryo-ken Hidari Koshi

62.
Kiba-Dachi
Hidari Jodan-Zuki

67.
Migi Zenkutsu-Dachi
Yama-Zuki

63.
Kiba-Dachi
Migi Chudan-Zuki

68a.
(turn counter clockwise)

68b.
Migi Kokutsu-Dachi
Migi Shuto-Uke

69.
Hidari Kokutsu-Dachi
Hidari Shuto-Uke

(step back with right foot)

70.
Musubi-Dachi
Migi Hou-Ken

71.
Yame

72.
Naore

汪輯

WANSHU

Chapter Fifteen
Wanshu

Alternate name: Wansu

Meaning of kata name: flying squirrel, pecking sparrow

From whom the author learned kata: Richard Lee

Lineage and history of kata: Tomari-Te

Wanshu is believed to have been influenced by old Northern Chinese martial arts where it first appeared in 1683, but the kata was originally taught by Tomari-Te master Kishin Teruya (1804-1864) to Maeda Pechin (1820-1890) to Chotoku Kyan (1870-1945).

The most commonly accepted theory about its creation and development is that Sappushi Wang Ji, an official from Xiuning, transmitted the kata while serving on Okinawa. Gichin Funakoshi changed the name to Enpi when he moved to Tokyo, Japan in 1922. Funakoshi changed the names of many Okinawan kata to sound like Japanese, in an effort to make the Okinawan art more palatable to the then nationalistic Japanese.

1.
Yoi

6.
Hidari Zenkutsu-Dachi
Hidari Gedan Barai

2.
Kamae
Musubi-Dachi

(left hand over right hand)

7.
Hidari Zenkutsu-Dachi
Migi Jodan Gyaku-Zuki

3.
Hajime
Musubi-Dachi

(right fist on left hand)

8.
Hidari Zenkutsu-Dachi
Migi Sukui-Uke

4.
Sanchin-Dachi
Hidari Gedan Shuto-Uke
Migi-ken koshi

9.
Hidari Zenkutsu-Dachi
Migi Jodan Shuto-Uchi

5.
Sanchin-Dachi
Migi Gedan-zuki
Hidari Soe-ken

10a.
Migi Chudan Mae-Geri

(chamber)

140

10b.
Migi Chudan Mae-Geri

14.
Hidari Zenkutsu-Dachi
Migi Jodan Gyaku-Zuki

10c.
Migi Chudan Mae-Geri

(chamber)

15.
Hidari Zenkutsu-Dachi
Migi Sukui-Uke

11.
Migi Kosa-Dachi
Migi-Ken Hiki-Uke
Hidari Shita-Zuki

16.
Hidari Zenkutsu-Dachi
Migi Jodan Shuto-Uchi

12.
Migi Kosa-Dachi
Migi Gedan Ura-ken
Hidari-ken Koshi

17a.
Migi Chudan Mae-Geri

(chamber)

13.
Hidari Zenkutsu-Dachi
Hidari Gedan Barai

17b.
Migi Chudan Mae-Geri

141

17c.
Migi Chudan Mae-Geri

(chamber)

22.
Hidari Zenkutsu-Dachi
Migi Sukui-Uke

18.
Migi Kosa-Dachi
Migi-Ken Hiki-Uke
Hidari Shita-Zuki

23.
Hidari Zenkutsu-Dachi
Migi Jodan Shuto-Uchi

19.
Migi Kosa-Dachi
Migi Gedan Ura-ken
Hidari-ken Koshi

24a.
Migi Chudan Mae-Geri

(chamber)

20.
Hidari Zenkutsu-Dachi
Hidari Gedan Barai

24b.
Migi Chudan Mae-Geri

21.
Hidari Zenkutsu-Dachi
Migi Jodan Gyaku-Zuki

24c.
Migi Chudan Mae-Geri

(chamber)

25.
Migi Kosa-Dachi
Migi-Ken Hiki-Uke
Hidari Shita-Zuki

29b.
Migi Chudan Mae-Geri

26.
Migi Kosa-Dachi
Migi Gedan Ura-ken
Hidari-ken Koshi

29b.
Migi Chudan Mae-Geri
Migi Hiki-Te

(chamber)

27.
Hidari Zenkutsu-Dachi
Hidari Gedan Barai

(turn counter clockwise 180
degrees)

30.
Migi Zenkutsu-Dachi
Migi Chudan Tate-Zuki

28.
Hidari Zenkutsu-Dachi
Migi Jodan Hira-Nuki-Te
Hidari-Soe-Te

31.
Migi Neko-Ashi-Dachi
Migi Saguri-Te

(step back with right foot)

29a.
Migi Chudan Mae-Geri

(chamber)

32.
Migi Zenkutsu-Dachi
Moro-te Shotei-Uke

(step left forward 45 degrees
with right foot)

143

33.
Hidari Zenkutsu-Dachi
Ryo-te Migi Koshi

(turn counter clockwise 180 degrees)

37b.
Yame

34.
Migi Zenkutsu-Dachi
Moro-te Shotei-Uke

(step forward with right foot)

38.
Naore

35.
Migi Kokutsu-Dachi
Migi Shuto-Uke

(turn counter clockwise, step back with left foot)

36.
Hidari Kokutsu-Dachi
Hidari Shuto-Uke

(step back with right foot)

37a.
Yame
Musubi-Dachi

(right fist on left hand)

王冠

WANKUAK

145

Chapter Sixteen
Wan Kuak

Alternate names: Wankan, ShoFu, Matsukaze

Meaning of kata name: king's crown or emperor's crown

From whom the author learned kata: Richard 'Biggie' Kim

Lineage and history of kata: Tomari-Te

Wan Kuak is practiced in many karate styles. Not much is known about the history of this kata. It originates from the Tomari-Te school and in modern karate is practiced in Shorin-Ryu, Shotokan, Shito-Ryu, and Matsubayashi-Ryu. Gichin Funakoshi once called it "ShoFu"; Kenwa Mabuni named it "Matsukaze".

1.
Yoi

6.
Kiba-Dachi
Ryo-ken Gedan-Barai

(heels out into Kiba-Dachi)

2.
Kamae

(left hand over right hand and heels together)

7.
Migi Kokutsu-Dachi
Migi Shuto-Uke

3.

(bring fists up front, knees bent, drop your body)

8.
Hidai Kokutsu-Dachi
Hidari Shuto-Uke

4.
Sanchin-Dachi

(cross arms, heels out into Sanchin-Dachi)

9.
Hidari Zenkutsu-Dachi
Moro-te Sashi-te

5.
Shiko-Dachi

(toes out into Shiko-Dachi)

10.
Kiba-Dachi
Ryo-ken Koshi

148

11.
Kiba-Dachi
Migi Jodan-Zuki

16.
Migi Zenkutsu-Dachi
Ryo-ken Mune-mae

12.
Kiba-Dachi
Hidari Chudan-Zuki

17.
Migi Zenkutsu-Dachi
Moro-te Ura-ken Yoko-Uchi

13.
Kiba-Dachi
Migi Chudan-Zuki

18.
Hidai Kokutsu-Dachi
Hidari Shuto-Uke

(step forward with left foot)

14.
Migi Nami-Ashi
Ryo-ken Koshi

19.
Migi Zenkutsu-Dachi
Migi Shuto-Uke

(step forward with right foot)

15.
Migi Zenkutsu-Dachi
Jodan Juji-Shuto-Uke

(step forward with right foot)

20.
Hidai Kokutsu-Dachi
Hidari Shuto-Uke

(step forward with left foot)

21.
Ushiro Sagi-Ashi-Dachi
Migi Uchi-Uke
Hidari-te Soe-te

26.
Hidari Zenkutsu-Dachi
Hidari gedan-Barai

(turn counter clockwise
step forward with left foot)

22.
Migi Han-mi Zenkutsu
-Dachi
Hidari Chudan-Zuki

27.
Hidari Zenkutsu-Dachi
Migi Chudan Gyaku-Zuki

23.
Shizen-Dachi
Migi Chudan-Zuki
Hidari-ken Shita

28.
Migi Kokutsu-Dachi
Migi Shuto-Uke

(step forward with right foot)

24.
Shizen-Dachi
Hidari Hai-shu Uke
Migi-ken Koshi

29.
Hidai Kokutsu-Dachi
Hidari Shuto-Uke

(step forward with left foot)

25. (Kiai)
Shizen-Dachi
Migi Chudan-Zuki
Migi-shou Ue

30.
Ushiro Sagi-Ashi-Dachi
Migi Uchi-Uke
Hidari-te Soe-te

31.
Migi Han-mi Zenkutsu
-Dachi
Hidari Chudan-Zuki

32.
Shizen-Dachi
Migi Chudan-Zuki
Hidari-ken Shita*

(*left fist below right arm)

33.
Shizen-Dachi
Hidari Hai-shu Uke
Migi-ken Koshi

34. (Kiai)
Shizen-Dachi
Migi Chudan-Zuki
Hidari-Shou Ue*

(*left palm up, over right arm)

35.
Hidari Zenkutsu-Dachi
Hidari Gedan-Barai

(turn counter clockwise
step forward with left foot)

36.
Migi Zenkutsu-Dachi
Migi Chudan oi-Zuki

(step forward with right foot)

37.
Hidari Zenkutsu-Dachi
Hidari Gedan-Barai

(turn counter clockwise
180 degrees)

38.
Hidari Zenkutsu-Dachi
Migi Chudan Gyaku-Zuki

39a.
Migi Chudan Mae-Geri

(chamber)

39b.
Migi Chudan Mae-Geri

39c.
Migi Chudan Mae-Geri

(chamber)

42.
Hidari Zenkutsu-Dachi
Migi Chudan oi-Zuki

(step forward with left foot)

40.
Migi Zenkutsu-Dachi
Hidari Chudan oi-Zuki

(step forward with right foot)

43a.
Migi Chudan Mae-Geri

(chamber)

41a.
Hidari Chudan Mae-Geri

(chamber)

43b.
Migi Chudan Mae-Geri

41b.
Hidari Chudan Mae-Geri

43c.
Migi Chudan Mae-Geri

(chamber)

41c.
Hidari Chudan Mae-Geri

(chamber)

44.

(step forward with right foot,
then turn around clockwise)

152

45.
Kiba-Dachi
Migi Uchi-Ude Barai

46.
Kiba-Dachi
Migi-ken Jodan Gamae

47.
Yame

48.
Naore

CHATAN-YARA KUSHANKU

Chapter Seventeen
Chatanyara Kushanku

Alternate names: Chatanyara Kusanku, Yara Kushanku

Meaning of kata name: (originator's names)

From whom the author learned kata: Richard Lee

Lineage and history of kata: Shuri-Te

Chatanyara Kushanku originally came from Chotoku Kyan (1870-1945). He trained under Master Yara, who lived in Chatan village in Okinawa around 1930. This particular Yara was the great grandson, or other family member, of Chatan Yara (1668-1756), who arranged and recreated this form.

Chatan Yara aka Yomitan Yara, is credited with being one of the first to disseminate the art of "Te" throughout Okinawa. This Yara is most noted for teaching Takahara Pe-chin, who would later be the teacher of Kanga Sakugawa, the father of Okinawan martial arts. Depending on Sakugawa's birth date, Yara may have been his teacher also (based on the kata he taught).

1.
Yoi

5.
Migi-Naname-Zenkutsu -Dachi
Hidari Jodan Shu-to-Uke

(step right with right foot)

2.
Kamae
Musubi-Dachi

(left hand over right hand)

6.
Shizen-Dachi
Migi Jodan Shu-to-Uke
Hidari Gedan Sho-tei-Uke

(step back with right foot)

3.
Musubi-Dachi

(bring both hands up)

7.
Hidari-Naname-Zenkutsu -Dachi
Hidari Jodan Shu-to-Uke
Migi Gedan Sho-tei-Uke

(step left with left foot)

4a.
Musubi-Dachi

(open both hands side)

8.
Migi-Naname-Zenkutsu -Dachi
Migi Jodan Shu-to-Uke
Hidari Gedan Sho-tei-Uke

4b.
Musubi-Dachi

(bring both hands down, right Shu-to on left palm)

9.
Shizen-Dachi
Migi Jodan Shu-to-Uchi
Hidari-te Sukui-Uke

(step back with right foot)

10.
Shizen-Dachi
Hidari Jodan-Haito
Migi-ken Koshi

15.
Shizen-Dachi
Hidari Chudan-Zuki

11.
Shizen-Dachi
Migi Jodan-Zuki

16.
Shizen-Dachi
Hidari Chudan-Uchi-Uke

12.
Shizen-Dachi
Hidari Chudan-Zuki

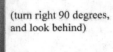

17.
Migi Neko-Ashi-Dachi
Ryo-ken Hidari-Koshi

(turn right 90 degrees,
and look behind)

13.
Shizen-Dachi
Migi Chudan-Zuki

18a.
Migi Chudan Mae-Geri

(chamber)

14.
Shizen-Dachi
Migi Chudan-Uchi-Uke

18b.
Migi Chudan Mae-Geri
Migi Tettsui-Uchi

18b. (side view)

22.
Migi Kokutsu-Dachi
Migi Shu-to-Uke

(step forward with right foot)

18c.
Migi Chudan Mae-Geri

(chamber)

23.
Migi Kokutsu-Dachi
Moro-te Sho-tei Age-Uke

19.
Hidari Kokutsu-Dachi
Hidari Shu-to-Uke

24.
Migi Kokutsu-Dachi
Moro-te Sho-tei Hiki-te

20.
Migi Kokutsu-Dachi
Migi Shu-to-Uke

(step forward with right foot)

25a.

(step forward with right foot)

21.
Hidari Kokutsu-Dachi
Hidari Shu-to-Uke

(step forward with left foot)

25b. (Kiai)
Migi Kokutsu-Dachi
Moro-te Sho-tei-Uchi

26.
Hidari Kiba-Dachi

(turn 180 degrees counter clockwise)

30.
Hidari Zenkutsu-Dachi
Migi Gedan Shita-Zuki
Hidari-ken Uchi-Uke

(step forward with left foot)

27.
Hidari Kiba-Dachi
Hidari Hai-to

31.
Hidari Shizen-Dachi
Migi Shu-to Soe-te

(step back with left foot)

27. (side view)

32.
Hidari Shizen-Dachi
Migi Shu-to Gedan Osae-Uke

28.
Migi Kiba-Dachi
Migi Hiji-Uchi
Hidari-Soe-te

(step forward with right foot)

33.
Hidari Shizen-Dachi
Migi Shu-to Jodan-Uke
Hidari-te Sukui-Uke

29.
Hidari Kiba-Dachi
Migi Jodan-Uke
Hidari Gedan-Barai

(look to left)

34.
Hidari Kosa-Dachi
Migi Jodan Shu-to-Uchi
Hidari Kake-te-Uke

34. (side view)

36. (side view)

35a.
Migi Chudan Mae-Geri

(chamber)

37.
Hidari Zenkutsu-Dachi
Migi Gedan Shita-Zuki
Hidari-ken Uchi-Uke

(step forward with left foot)

35b.
Migi Chudan Mae-Geri

38.
Hidari Shizen-Dachi
Migi Shu-to Gedan Osae-Uke

35c.
Migi Chudan Mae-Geri

(chamber)

39.
Hidari Kosa-Dachi
Migi Jodan Shu-to-Uchi
Hidari Kake-te-Uke

36.
Hidari Kiba-Dachi
Migi Jodan-Uke
Hidari Gedan-Barai

(look to left)

40a.
Migi Chudan Mae-Geri

(chamber)

40b.
Migi Chudan Mae-Geri

44.

(lift right knee up. turn left
counter clockwise)

40c.
Migi Chudan Mae-Geri

(chamber)

45.
Hidari Kokutsu-Dachi
Hidari Chudan Uchi-Uke

41.
Hidari Kiba-Dachi
Migi Jodan-Uke
Hidari Gedan-Barai

(look to left)

46a.
Hidari Chudan Mae-Geri

(chamber)

42.
Hidari Zenkutsu-Dachi
Migi Gedan Shita-Zuki
Hidari-ken Uchi-Uke

(step forward with left foot)

46b.
Migi Chudan Mae-Geri

43.
Hidari Shizen-Dachi
Migi Shu-to Gedan Osae-Uke

(step back with left foot)

46c.
Hidari Chudan Mae-Geri

(chamber)

163

47.
Hidari Zenkutsu-Dachi
Migi Hiji-Uchi
Hidari Soe-te

50c.
Hidari Chudan Mae-Geri

(chamber)

48.

(lift right knee up. turn left
counter clockwise)

51.
Migi Zenkutsu-Dachi
Hidari Hiji-Uchi
Migi Soe-te

49.
Migi Kokutsu-Dachi
Migi Chudan Uchi-Uke

52.
Hidari Kokutsu-Dachi
Hidari Shu-to-Uke

(turn 180 degrees counter clock
-wise)

50a.
Hidari Chudan Mae-Geri

(chamber)

53.
Migi Kokutsu-Dachi
Migi Shu-to-Uke

(step forward 45 degrees)

50b.
Hidari Chudan Mae-Geri

54.
Migi Kokutsu-Dachi
Migi Shu-to-Uke

(turn 135 degrees clockwise)

55.
Hidari Kokutsu-Dachi
Hidari Shu-to-Uke

(step forward 45 degrees)

56a.

(step back with left foot)

56b.
Kiba-Dachi
Moro-te Shu-to Gedan
Juji-Uke

57.
Hidari Kiba-Dachi
Migi Jodan Shu-to-Uke
Hidari Gedan Shu-to-Uke

(look to left)

58.
Hidari Kosa-Dachi
Hidari-te Sukui-Uke

59.
Hidari Kosa-Dachi
Migi Jodan Shu-to-Uchi
Hidari Mawashi-kake-Uke

60a.
Migi Chudan Mae-Geri

(chamber)

60b.
Migi Chudan Mae-Geri

60c.
Migi Chudan Mae-Geri
Moro-te Jodan Shu-to
Juji-Uke

(chamber)

61.
Migi Kosa-Dachi
Migi Jodan Ura-Ken-Uchi

62.
Migi Zenkutsu-Dachi
Migi Uchi-Uke

66b.
Migi Fuse-Mi

63.
Migi Zenkutsu-Dachi
Hidari Chudan-Zuki

67a.
Hidari Ka-sei Ashi-barai

(change hands position)

64.
Migi Zenkutsu-Dachi
Migi Chudan-Zuki

67b.
Hidari Ka-sei Ashi-barai

65.
Migi Nami-Ashi
Hidari Soe-te

(hit left palm with sole of
right foot)

67c.
Hidari Ka-sei Ashi-barai

66a.
(turn 180 degrees, drop
right foot and body down)

68.
Hidari Kiba-Dachi

69a.
Tobi-Koshi

(jump up, both knees high)

73.
Migi Zenkutsu-Dachi
Migi Chudan Nuki-te

(step forward with right foot)

69b.

(landing)

74.
Migi Kokutsu-Dachi
Migi Jodan Sho-tei-Uke

70. (Kiai)
Kiba-Dachi
Ryo-ken Gedan-Zuki

75.

(turn 180 degrees counter
clockwise, step forward with
left foot)

71.
Hidari Kokutsu-Dachi
Migi Gedan Nuki-te
Hidari-te Sukui-Uke

76.
Hidari Kiba-Dachi
Hidari Jodan Ura-Ken

72.
Hdari Kokutsu-Dachi
Hidari Shu-to Gedan-Barai

77.
Hidari Kiba-Dachi
Hidari-ken Uchi-Uke

78.
Hirari Kiba-Dachi
Hidari Tettsui-Uchi

80d.
Migi Neko-Ashi-Dachi
Mawashi-Uke

(complete)

79.
Hidari Zenkutsu-Dachi
Migi Hiji-Uchi
Hidari-Soe-te

81.
Migi Neko-Ashi-Dachi
Mawashi-Uke

(look to right)

80a.
Migi Neko-Ashi-Dachi
Mawashi-Uke

(look to right and step left with right foot into Neko-Ashi)

82.
Migi Kiba-Dachi
Migi gedan barai
Hidari Jodan Ura-Ken

(step right with right foot into Kiba-Dachi)

80b.
Migi Neko-Ashi-Dachi
Mawashi-Uke

82. (side view)

80c.
Migi Neko-Ashi-Dachi
Mawashi-Uke

83.
Kiba-Dachi
Hidari Soto-Uke

(step forward with left foot into Kiba-Dachi)

84.
Kiba-Dachi
Migi Uchi-Uke

(slide step forward with left foot
then right foot, into Kiba-Dachi)

89.
Migi Neko-Ashi-Dachi
Ryo-ken Chudan Juji-Uke

(step back with right foot)

85.
Koba-Dachi
Ryo-ken Gedan Juji-Uke

90.
Migi Chudan Hiza-Uke

86.
Shizen-Dachi
Jodan Shu-to Juji-Uke

91a.
Nidan-Geri
(Hidari Tobi-Mae-Geri)

(chamber)

87.

(turn clockwise with left foot
first then right foot)

91b.
Nidan-Geri
(Hidari Tobi-Mae-Geri)

88.
Migi Zenkutsu-Dachi
Ryo-ken Chudan Juji-Uke

91c.
Nidan-Geri
(Hidari Tobi-Mae-Geri)

(chamber)

169

91d
Nidan-Deri
(Migi Tobi-Mae-Geri)

(chamber)

94.
Hidari Kokutsu-Dachi
Migi Jodan Ura-ken
Hidari Gedan Barai

(step forward with left foot)

91e
Nidan-Geri
(Migi Tobi-Mae-Geri)

95.

(look to right)

91f
Nidan-Geri
(Migi Tobi-Mae-Geri)

(chamber)

96.
Migi-Shuto Sukui-Uke
Hidari Chudan Nuki-te

(half step right with left foot))

92. (Kiai)
Migi Zenkutsu-Dachi
Migi Ura-ken-Uchi

97.
Migi Kokutsu-Dachi
Migi Shuto-Uke

93.
Hidari Neko-Ashi-Dachi
Migi-ken Gedan,
Hidari-ken Jodan Kamae

(turn 180 degrees counter
clockwise)

98.
Yame

松村抜砦

MATSUMURA-PASSAI

171

Chapter Eighteen
Matsumura Passai

Alternate name: Shuri Patsai

Meaning of kata name: extract from a fortress, remove an obstruction

From whom the author learned kata: Richard 'Biggie' Kim

Lineage and history of kata: Shuri-Te

The original Passai kata, as practiced by Sokon Matsumura (1809-1899) and most Shuri samurais, was called Oyadomari no Passai and named after Tomari-Te karate master Kokan Oyadomari (1827-1905). Later named Passai of Anko Itosu (1831-1915), who popularized karate by introducing it into the curriculum of Okinawan schools.

There are several variations, including Passai Sho (minor) and Passai Dai (major). The Okinawans did not have a clear definition for the name "Passai" for Funakoshi to translate into Japanese, so he substituted it with a similar sounding word in Kanji, "Bassai". Passai is thought to be in reference to the power with which the kata should be executed, emphasizing energy generation from the hips and waist. However, the designation of Bassai by the Japanese does not appear to have a direct relation to movements in the kata or its origins. Nowadays, Passai kata is usually classified as intermediate, but in Okinawa it is one of the most important and very difficult to practice advanced forms.

1.
Yoi

6.
Migi Kosa-Dachi
Migi Chudan Uchi-Uke
Hidari Soe-te

2.
Kamae
Musubi-Dachi
Migi Gedan Hou-Ken

(step right foot to left foot,
hold right fist with left hand)

7.
Migi Neko Ashi-Dachi
Ryo-te Koshi

(turn clockwise 180 degrees,
then step forward with right foot)

3.
(bring left foot up slowly)

8.
Migi Neko-Ashi-Dachi
Moro-te Jodan-Shuto-Uke

4.
Hidari Neko-Ashi-Dachi
Migi Gedan Hou-Ken

(step forward with left foot)

9.
Migi Neko-Ashi-Dachi
Migi Jodan-Uke
Hidari-ken Koshi

5.
Migi Fumi-Komi

10.
Hidari Kokutsu-Dachi
Migi Otoshi-Uke
Hidari Shita-Zuki

(step forward with left foot)

174

10a. (side view)

15.

(step back with right foot)

11.
Migi Neko-Ashi-Dachi
Migi-ken Jodan
Hidari-ken Chudan

(turn 180 degrees counter
clockwise)

16.
Migi Uchi-Ude Sukui-Uke
Hidari-ken Soe

(turn counter clockwise
90 degrees)

12.
Migi Neko-Ashi-Dachi
Hidari Jodan-Uke
Migi-ken Koshi

17.
Shizen-Dachi
Migi-ken Jodan-Sukui-Age

13.

(step forward with right foot)

18.
Hidari Kokutsu-Dachi
Hidari-ken Shita-Zuki
Migi-ken Otoshi-Uke

(step forward with left foot)

14.
Migi Neko-Ashi-Dachi
Migi-ken Shita-Zuki
Hidari-ken Otoshi-Uke

19.
Hidari Kokutsu-Dachi
Hidari Jodan-Uke
Migi-ken Koshi

20.
Migi Kokutsu-Dachi
Migi-ken Shita-Zuki
Hidari-ken Otoshi-Uke

(step forward with right foot)

25.
Shizen-Dachi
Migi Chudan Uchi-Uke

21.
Migi Kosa-Dachi
Moro-te Jodan Shuto-Uke

(step forward with left foot)

26.
Shizen-Dachi
Hidari Chudan-Zuki

22.
Shizen-Dachi
Ryo-ken Migi-Koshi

(step side with left foot)

27.
Shizen-Dachi
Hidari Chudan-Uke

23.
Shizen-Dachi
Hidari Sashi-te

28.
Hidari Chudan Sashi-te
Migi-te Uchi-Uke

24.
Shizen-Dachi
Migi Chudan-Zuki

29.
Migi Kokutsu-Dachi
Migi Gedan Shuto-Uke

30.
Hidari Kokutsu-Dachi
Hidari Gedan Shuto-Uke

(step forward with left foot)

35.

(put right foot down, then turn
270 degrees counter clockwise)

31.
Migi Kokutsu-Dachi
Migi Gedan Shuto-Uke

(step forward with right foot)

36.
Hidari Neko-Ashi-Dachi
Hidari Ura-Ashi-Kake
Hidari Kake-te-Uke

32.
Hidari Kokutsu-Dachi
Hidari Chudan Shuto-Uke

(step back with right foot)

37.
Hidari Neko-Ashi-Dachi
Hidari Kake-te-Uke

33.
Hidari Zenkutsu-Dachi
Moro-te Jodan Hira-Nuki-te

38.

(turn 180 degrees clockwise)

34.
Migi-Hiza-Ate

39.
Migi Neko-Ashi-Dachi
Migi Ura-Ashi-Kake
Migi Kake-te-Uke

177

40.
Migi Neko-Ashi-Dachi
Migi Kake-te-Uke

45.

(put right knee up high, and
open both fists to side)

41.

(turn 90 degrees counter
clockwise)

46.
Migi Zenkutsu-Dachi
Ryo-ken Hasami-Uchi

42.
Migi Neko-Ashi-Dachi
Migi Ura-Ashi-Kake
Migi Kake-te-Uke

46a. (side view)

43.
Migi Neko-Ashi-Dachi
Ryo-te Koshi

47.

(step forward with left foot,
both fists are left side)

44.
Migi Neko-Ashi-Dachi
Ryo-te Shuto Jodan-Uke

47a. (side view)

48.
Migi Zenkutsu-Dachi
Ryo-Ken Chudan-Zuki

52.
Hidari Neko-Ashi-Dachi
Hidari Hai-to-Uke

48a. (side view)

52a. (side view)

49.
Hidari Kokutsu-Dachi
Migi Jodan-Ura-Ken
Hidari Gedan-Barai

(turn 180 degrees counter clockwise)

53.
Migi Mikazuki-Geri

50.
Migi Kosa-Dachi
Hidari Jodan-Ura-Ken
Migi Gedan-Barai

(step forward with right foot)

53a. (side view)

51.
Hidari Neko-Ashi-Dachi
Ryo-ken Migi-Koshi

(turn 90 degrees counter clockwise, step forward with left foot)

54.
Migi Neko-Ashi-Dachi
Ryo-ken Jodan
Naka-Daka-Ippon-ken-Zuki

54a. (side view)

59.
Migi Neko-Ashi-Dachi
Ryo-ken Hidari Koshi

55
Migi Ura-Ashi-Kake

60.
Migi Neko-Ashi-Dachi
Ryo-ken Chudan-Zuki

56.
Migi Neko-Ashi-Dachi

60a. (side view)

57.
Migi Neko-Ashi-Dachi
Migi Jodan Naka-Daka
-Ippon-ken Yoi

61.

(step back with right foot)

58.
Migi Neko-Ashi-Dachi
Migi Jodan Naka-Daka
-Ippon-ken Uchi

62.
Hidari Hei-soku-Dachi
Ryo-ken Migi Koshi

63a.
Hidari-Chudan-Mae-Geri
Ryo-ken Koshi

(chamber)

65.
Migi Hei-soku-Dachi
Ryo-ken Hidari Koshi

63b.
Hidari-Chudan-Mae-Geri
Ryo-ken Koshi

66.
Migi Neko-Ashi-Dachi
Ryo-ken Hidari Koshi

63c.
Hidari-Chudan-Mae-Geri
Ryo-ken Koshi

(chamber)

67a.
Migi Chudan-Mae-Geri
Ryo-ken Hidari Koshi

(chamber)

64.
Hidari Zenkutsu-Dachi
Yama-Zuki

67b.
Migi Chudan-Mae-Geri
Ryo-ken Hidari Koshi

64a. (side view)

67c.
Migi Chudan-Mae-Geri
Ryo-ken Hidari Koshi

(chamber)

181

68.
Migi Zenkutsu-Dachi
Yama-Zuki

73.
Migi Naname Zenkutsu
-Dachi
Hidari Uchi-Ude Barai

69.

(turn 180 degrees counter clockwise, step left foot to side)

74.
Migi Naname Zenkutsu
-Dachi
Hidari Ura-ken Otoshi-Uchi

70.
Hidari Naname Zenkutsu
-Dachi
Migi Uchi-Ude Barai

75.
Hidari Ura-Ashi-Kake
Ryo-te Kosa Gamae

71.
Hidari Naname Zenkutsu
-Dachi
Migi Ura-ken Otoshi-Uchi

76.
Hidari Neko-Ashi-Dachi
Hidari Kake-te-Uke

72.
Migi Naname Zenkutsu
-Dachi

(shift body to right)

77.
Migi Ura-Ashi-Kake
Ryo-te Kosa-Gamae

78.
Migi Neko-Ashi-Dachi
Migi Kake-te-Uke

79.
Yame
Musubi-Dachi
Migi Hou-Ken

(step back with right foot,
hold right fist with left hand)

80.
Musubi-Dachi
Migi Hou-Ken

(look front)

81.
Naore

屋部鎭闘

YABU CHINTO

Chapter Nineteen
Yabu Chinto

Alternate name: Chinto

Meaning of kata name: fighting to the east

From whom the author learned kata: Richard 'Biggie' Kim

Lineage and history of kata: Tomari-Te

When Gichin Funakoshi brought karate to Japan, he changed the name of Chintō to Gankaku (meaning "crane on a rock"), possibly to avoid anti-Chinese sentiment of the time. He also modified the actual pattern of movement, or embusen, to a layout similar to other Shotokan kata.

According to legend, it is named after a Chinese sailor, sometimes referred to as Chinto, whose ship crashed on the Okinawan coast. To survive, Chintō stole from the crops of local people. Later he met local martial artists like Gusukuma, Kinjo and Kosaku Matsumora, and proceeded to teach them his martial arts.

This "Yabu-Chinto" is old and might be one of the original versions that were practiced by Kentsu Yabu (1866-1937).

1.
Yoi

6.

(step back with right again)

2.
Kamae

(left hand over right hand, and heels together)

7.
Hidari Hanmi

(hands up slowly)

3.
Shizen-Dachi

(look to left, hands are at side)

8.
Hidari Neko-Ashi-Dachi
Ryote Juji-Uke

4.

(step back with right foot)

9a.
Hidari Neko-Ashi-Dachi
Ryote-Ude-Tori

5.

(step back with left foot)

9b.
Hidari Neko-Ashi-Dachi
Ryote-Ude-Tori

10.
Hidari Neko-Ashi-Dachi
Ryoken Migi-Koshi

(left fist over right fist)

14.
Hidari Zenkutsu-Dachi
Hidari Gedan-Barai

11.
Hidari Neko-Ashi-Dachi
Hidari Yoko-Tettsui

15.

(lift right knee up quickly,
and step back with right foot)

12.
Kiba-Dachi
Migi Kagi-Zuki

16.
Hidari Shizen-Tai

13a.

(turn to right)

17.

(step back with left foot)

13b.

(turning 360 degree,
step forward with left foot)

18.
Hidari Shizen-Tai

(step back with right foot)

189

19.
Hidari Neko-Ashi-Dachi

(hands move up slowly)

22b.
Nidan-Geri

(right front snap kick)

20.
Hidari Neko-Ashi-Dachi
Ryote Juji-Uke

22c.
Nidan-Geri

(continue)

21.
Hidari Neko-Ashi-Dachi
Ryoken-Uke

22d.
Nidan-Geri

(continue)

22.
Ryoken-Uke
Hidari Hiza-Uke

22e.
Nidan-Geri

(left front snap kick)

23a.
Nidan-Geri

(step forward with left foot,
then jump with right foot)

22f.
Nidan-Geri

(continue)

23.

(step forward with left foot)

26.
Migi Zenkutsu-Dachi
Migi Yoko-Tettsui-Uchi

24.
Hidari Zenkutsu-Dachi
Ryoken Gedan-Juji-Uke

27.
Hidari Zenkutsu-Dachi
Hidari Chudan-Oi-Zuki

25a.

(turn counter clockwise, 225 degrees)

28.
Hidari Zenkutsu-Dachi
Migi Hiji-Ate

25b.

(continue)

29.
Hidari Zenkutsu-Dachi
Ryote Gedan-Sukui-Uke

25c.

(continue)

30a.
Ryote Jodan-Sukui-Uke

(step forward with right foot)

30b.
Ryote Jodan-Sukui-Uke

(continue)

34.
Migi Zenkutsu-Dachi
Ryote-Shuto-Uchi

31a.

(continue)

35.
Migi Zenkutsu-Dachi
Migi Jodan-Nukite

31b.
Kiba-Dachi
Ryote Shuto
Jodan-Mawashi-Uchi

36.
Migi Zenkutsu-Dachi

(continue, cross arms)

32.

(step back with right foot, then left foot)

37.
Migi Zenkutsu-Dachi
Moro-te Gedan-Uke

33.
Migi Zenkutsu-Dachi

(continue, hands behind head)

38.
Migi Zenkutsu-Dachi
Hidari-te Osae-Uke

(right hand under left arm)

39.
Migi Zenkutsu-Dachi
Migi Tate-Shuto-Uke

44.
Hidari Kosa-Dachi
Ryoken Uchi-Uke

40.
Migi Zenkutsu-Dachi
Hidari Jodan-Hiji-Uchi

45.
Hidari Kosa-Dachi
Ryoken Gedan-Uke

41.
Migi Zenkutsu-Dachi
Ryote Jodan Osae-Uke

46.
Migi Neko-Ashi-Dachi
Moro-te Nukite

(turn right 180 degrees)

42.
Migi Hiza-Ate

47a.
Migi Mae-Geri
Ryoken Koshi

(chamber)

43.
Hidari Kosa-Dachi
Ryote Gedan Osae-Uke

47b.
Migi Mae-Geri

(right front snap kick)

47c.
Migi Mae-Geri
Ryoken Koshi

(chamber)

50b.
Kiba-Dachi
Ryoken Gedan-Barai

48.
Kiba-Dachi
Ryoken Koshi

51a.

(step forward with left foot)

49a.
Kiba-Dachi

(fists move up slowly)

51b.
Hidari Fudo-Dachi
Hidari-ken-Gedan,
Migi-ken-Jodan no Kamae

49b.
Kiba-Dachi
Ryoken Uchi-Uke

52.
Migi Fudo-Dachi
Migi-ken-Gedan,
Hidari-ken-Jodan no Kamae

50a.
Kiba-Dachi

(fists move down slowly)

53a.

(turn counter clock wise,
then step with left foot)

53b.
Hidari Fudo-Dachi
Hidari-ken-Gedan,
Migi-ken-Jodan no Kamae

57.
Shizen-tai
Ryoken Koshi

54.
Hidari Kosa-Dachi
Ryoken Gedan Juji-Uke

58.
Migi Hiji-Uke

55.
Hidari Kosa-Dachi
Ryoken Chudan-Uchi-Uke

59.
Hidari Hiji-Uke

56a.

(turn right,
move fists up slowly)

60.
Migi Kosa-Dachi
Ryote Nukite

56b.
Shizen-tai

(fists move down slowly)

61a.
Hidari Mae-Geri

(chamber)

195

61b.
Hidari Mae-Geri

(left front snap kick)

64-front view.

61c.
Hidari Mae-Geri

(chamber)

65.
Kiba-Dachi
Ryote Jodan Sashi-te

62.
Hidari Zenkutsu-Dachi
Hidari Sashi-te

66.
Hidari Kosa-Dachi
Ryote Gedan Harai-Uke

63.
Migi Zenkutsu-Dachi
Migi Chudan Oi-Zuki

67.
Hidari Kosa-Dachi
Ryote Nukite

64. Kiai
Kiba-Dachi
Ryoken Kagi-Zuki

68a.
Migi Mae-Geri

(chamber)

68b.
Migi Mae-Geri

(right front snap kick)

72a.
Hidari Mae-Geri

(chamber)

68c.
Migi Mae-Geri

(chamber)

72b.
Hidari Mae-Geri

(left front snap kick)

69.
Migi Zenkutsu-Dachi
Ryote Jodan Sashi-te

72c.
Hidari Mae-Geri

(chamber)

70.
Migi Kosau-Dachi
Ryote Gedan Harai-Uke

73.
Hidari Zenkutu-Dachi
Hidari Tate-Shuto-Uke

71.
Migi Kosau-Dachi
Ryote Jodan Sashi-te

74a.
Migi Tate-Hiji-Uchi
Migi Hiza-Uke

(chamber)

74b.
Migi Mae-Geri

(right front snap kick)

76c.
Kiba-Dachi
Migi Shotei-Osae

74c.
Migi Mae-Geri

(chamber)

77.

(step back with right foot very quickly)

75.
Migi Tate-Hiza
Hidari-Otoshi-Zuki

78.
Kiba-Dachi

(step back with left foot very quickly)

76a.
Kiba-Dachi

(open right hand)

79.
Yame

76b.
Kiba-Dachi

(move right hand down slowly)

80.
Naore

YABU USESHI

199

Chapter Twenty
Yabu Useishi

Alternate name: Gojyushiho

Meaning of kata name: fifty four steps

From whom the author learned kata: Richard 'Biggie' Kim

Lineage and history of kata: Shuri -Te

Gojūshiho Shō and Gojūshiho Dai are two versions in Shotokan that come from a single Shorin-Ryu kata called Useishi (54) or Gojūshiho. Originally, Yabu Useichi was transported or created by Sokon Matsumura (1809-1899) who studied martial arts when he was in Beijing.

Yabu-Useshi kata was practiced by Kentsu Yabu (1866-1937). The kata might be the original Useishi that came directly from Sokon Matsumura.

1.
Yoi

6.
Hidari Zenkutsu-Dachi
Ryo-ken Koshi

2.
Hidari Sho-tei Osae
Migi-ken Koshi

(step forward with right foot)

6.
Hidari Zenkutsu-Dachi
Ryo-ken Jodan Mawashi
-Uchi

3.
Migi Zenkutsu-Dachi
Migi Chudan Shita-Zuki
Hidari-ken Soe

7.
Migi Zenkutsu-Dachi
Ryo-ken Koshi

(step 45 degrees forward with
right foot)

4.
Hidari Neko-Ashi-Dahi
Ryo-ken Koshi

(step forward with left foot)

7.
Migi Zenkutsu-Dachi
Jodan Shuto-Juji-Uke

5.
Hidari Zenkutsu-Dachi
Jodan Shuto-Juji-Uke

8.
Migi Zenkutsu-Dachi
Ryo-ken Koshi

9.
Hidari Zenkutsu-Dachi
Ryo-ken Jodan Mawashi
-Uchi

14a.
Migi Chudan-Mae-Geri

(chamber)

10.
Hidari Shuto Nagashi-Uke
Migi-ken Mae

(step 45 degrees forward with
left foot)

14b.
Migi Chudan-Mae-Geri

11.
Hidari Zenkutsu-Dachi
Hidari Tate-Shuto-Uke
Migi-ken Koshi

14c.
Migi Chudan-Mae-Geri

(chamber)

12.
Hidari Zenkutsu-Dachi
Migi Chudan Gyaku-Zuki

15.
Hidari Zenkutsu-Dachi
Migi Gedan Gyaku-Zuki

13.
Hidari Zenkutsu-Dachi
Hidari Chudan-Zuki

16.
Migi Neko-Ashi-Dachi
Migi Shuto Nagashi-Uke
Hidari-ken Koshi

(step 45 degrees front with
right foot)

17.
Migi Zenkutsu-Dachi
Migi Shuto-Uchi-Uke
Hidari-ken Mae

21b.
Hidari Chudan-Mae-Geri

18.
Migi Zenkutsu-Dachi
Migi Tate-Shuto-Uke
Hidari-ken Koshi

21c.
Hidari Chudan-Mae-Geri

(chamber)

19.
Migi Zenkutsu-Dachi
Hidari Chudan-Gyaku-Zuki

22.
Migi Zenkutsu-Dachi
Hidari Gedan Gyaku-Zuki

20.
Migi Zenkutsu-Dachi
Migi Chudan-Zuki

23.
Kiba-Dachi
Migi Jodan Hiji-Uchi

21a.
Hidari Chudan-Mae-Geri

(chamber)

24.
Hidari Zenkutsu-Dachi
Hidari-te Sukui-Uke
Migi-te Osae

(step back with left foot, turn
180 degrees counter clockwise)

204

24a. (front view)

29.
Migi Zenkutsu-Dachi
Migi Chudan-Nuki-te
Hidari-Shuto Hidari-Koshi

(step forward with right foot)

25.
Migi Kokutsu-Dachi
Migi Shuto-Uke

(step forward with right foot)

30.
Musubi-Dachi
Hidari Chudan-Nuki-te
Migi-Shuto Migi-Koshi

(step back with right foot)

26.
Musubi-Dachi
Hidari Chudan-Nuki-te
Migi-Shuto Migi-Koshi

(step back with right foot)

31.
Migi Zenkutsu-Dachi
Migi Chudan-Nuki-te
Hidari-Shuto Hidari-Koshi

(step forward with right foot)

27.
Migi Zenkutsu-Dachi
Migi Chudan-Nuki-te
Hidari-Shuto Hidari-Koshi

(step forward with right foot)

32.
Migi Kokutsu-Dachi
Migi Shuto-Uke

(turn 180 degrees counter
clockwise, step forward with
right foot)

28.
Musubi-Dachi
Hidari Chudan-Nuki-te
Migi-Shuto Migi-Koshi

(step back with right foot)

33a.
Musubi-Dachi
Hidari Chudan-Nuki-te
Migi-Shuto Migi-Koshi

(step back with right foot)

33b.
Musubi-Dachi
Hidari Chudan-Nuki-te
Migi-Shuto Migi-Koshi

38.
Migi Zenkutsu-Dachi
Migi Chudan-Nuki-te
Hidari-Shuto Hidari-Koshi

(step forward with right foot)

34.
Migi Zenkutsu-Dachi
Migi Chudan-Nuki-te
Hidari-Shuto Hidari-Koshi

(step forward with right foot)

39.

(turn 90 degrees counter clockwise step side with left foot)

35.
Musubi-Dachi
Hidari Chudan-Nuki-te
Migi-Shuto Migi-Koshi

(step back with right foot)

40.
Hidari Jodan Hai-to
Migi Chudan-Soe-te

36.
Migi Zenkutsu-Dachi
Migi Chudan-Nuki-te
Hidari-Shuto Hidari-Koshi

(step forward with right foot)

41.
Migi Kokutsu-Dachi
Migi Jodan Hai-to
Hidari-te Shuto

37.
Musubi-Dachi
Hidari Chudan-Nuki-te
Migi-Shuto Migi-Koshi

(step back with right foot)

42.
Kiba-Dachi
Hidari Gedan-Hai-to
Migi-Shuto Soe-te

43.
Migi Kosa-Dachi

(step side with right foot)

48.
Kiba-Dachi
Hidari-Ushiro Jodan-Shuto
Migi Chudan-Shuto

44.
Hidari-Ashi Fumi-Komi
Ryo-te Jodan Sukui-Uke

49.
Kiba-Dachi
Migi Gedan-Hai-to
Hidari-Shuto Soe-te

45.
Hidari-Ashi Fumi-Komi
Migi Ushiro-Jodan-Shuto
Hidari Chudan-Shuto

50.
Hidari Kosa-Dachi

(step side with left foot)

46.
Kiba-Dachi
Hidari Gedan-Hai-to
Migi-Shuto Soe-te

(step side with left foot)

51.
Migi-Ashi Fumi-Komi
Ryo-te Jodan Sukui-Uke

47.
Kiba-Dachi
Migi Jodan Hai-to
Hidari-te Shuto

52.
Migi-Ashi Fumi-Komi
Hidari Ushiro-Jodan-Shuto
Migi Chudan-Shuto

207

53.
Kiba-Dachi
Migi Gedan-Hai-to
Hidari-Shuto Soe-te

(step side with right foot)

57.
Musubi-Dachi
Hidari Chudan-Nuki-te
Migi-Shuto Migi-Koshi

(step back with right foot)

54.
Migi Shuto-Uchi-Yoi

(step back with right foot)

59.
Migi Zenkutsu-Dachi
Migi Chudan Nuki-te
Hidari-Shuto Hidari-Koshi

(step forward with right foot)

55.
Migi Kokutsu-Dachi
Migi Shuto-Uke

(step forward with right foot)

60.
Musubi-Dachi
Hidari Chudan-Nuki-te
Migi-Shuto Migi-Koshi

(step back with right foot)

56.
Musubi-Dachi
Hidari Chudan-Nuki-te
Migi-Shuto Migi-Koshi

(step back with right foot)

61.
Migi Zenkutsu-Dachi
Migi Chudan Nuki-te
Hidari-Shuto Hidari-Koshi

(step forward with right foot)

57.
Migi Zenkutsu-Dachi
Migi Chudan Nuki-te
Hidari-Shuto Hidari-Koshi

(step forward with right foot)

62.
Hidarii Zenkutsu-Dachi
Migi Jodan Shuto-Uchi

(turn 180 degrees counter
clockwise)

208

63.
Migi Zenkutsu-Dachi
Migi Shuto Nagashi-Uke

68.
Migi Zenkutsu-Dachi
Migi Kei-kou-ken Uchi
-Otoshi

(step forward with right foot)

64.
Migi Zenkutsu-Dachi
Migi Jodan Shuto-Uchi

69.
Migi Zenkutsu-Dachi
Migi Kei-kou-ken Uchi-Age

65.
Migi Zenkutsu-Dachi
Hidari Jodan Shuto-Uchi

70a.
Hidari Chudan-Mae-Geri

(chamber)

66.
Hidari Zenkutsu-Dachi
Hidari Shuto Nagashi-Uke

(step forward with left foot)

70b.
Hidari Chudan-Mae-Geri

67.
Hidari Zenkutsu-Dachi
Hidari Jodan Shuto-Uchi

70c.
Hidari Chudan-Mae-Geri

(chamber)

71.
Migi Zenkutsu-Dachi
Migi-ken Nagashi-Uke
Hidari Gedan-Zuki

75.
Migi Zenkutsu-Dachi
Migi Chudan Nuki-te
Hidari-Shuto Hidari-Koshi

(step forward with right foot)

72.
Hidari Zenkutsu-Dachi
Hidari Jodan Hiji-Uchi
Migi Ushiro-Gedan-Barai

(turn 180 degrees counter clockwise)

76.
Musubi-Dachi
Hidari Chudan-Nuki-te
Migi-Shuto Migi-Koshi

(step back with right foot)

72a. (side view)

77.
Migi Zenkutsu-Dachi
Migi Chudan Nuki-te
Hidari-Shuto Hidari-Koshi

(step forward with right foot)

73.
Migi Kokutsu-Dachi
Migi Shuto-Uke

(step forward with right foot)

78.
Musubi-Dachi
Hidari Chudan-Nuki-te
Migi-Shuto Migi-Koshi

(step back with right foot)

74.
Musubi-Dachi
Hidari Chudan-Nuki-te
Migi-Shuto Migi-Koshi

(step back with right foot)

79.
Migi Zenkutsu-Dachi
Migi Chudan Nuki-te
Hidari-Shuto Hidari-Koshi

(step forward with right foot)

80a.
(turn 180 degrees counter clockwise)

84.
Kiba-Dachi
Migi Shuto-Uchi-Nagashi

80b.
Kiba-Dachi
Hidari Gedan Shuto-Uchi
Migi-ken Koshi

(step side with left foot)

85.
Kiba-Dachi
Migi-Shuto Gedan-Barai

81.
Migi Kosa-Dachi

(step side with right foot)

86.
Hidari Kosa-Dachi

(step side with left foot)

82.
Hidari-Ashi Fumi-Komi

87.
Migi-Ashi Fumi-Komi

83.
Kiba-Dachi
Migi Chudan-Nuki-te
Hidari-Hiji-Uke

(step side with left foot)

88.
Kiba-Dachi
Migi Chudan Nuki-te
Hidari-Hiji-Uke

(step side with right foot)

89.
Hidari-te Osae-Uke

(step half to right)

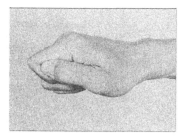

93a. (Ippon-Ken)

90.
Migi Zenkutsu-Dachi
Migi-ken Shita-Zuki
Hidari-ken-Osae

(step forward with right foot)

94.
Hei-ko-Dachi
Ryo-Hiji Suihei

91.
Migi Kiba-Dachi
Hidari Yoko-Tettsui

(step back with right foot)

95.
Hei-ko-Dachi
Ryo-Ura-ken Suihei-Uchi

92. (Kiai)
Migi Zenkutsu-Dachi
Migi Chudan-Oi-Zuki

(step forward with right foot)

96.
Hidari Zenkutsu-Dachi
Migi-Hiji Yoko-Uchi
Hidari Ushiro-Hiji-Ate

93.
Hei-ko-Dachi
Ryo Ippon-Ken Mae

(turn 90 degrees counter clockwise)

96a. (side view)

212

97.
Migi-Neko-Ashi-Dachi
Moro-te Gedan Hai-to

(step forward with right foot)

101.
Migi Neko-Ashi-Dachi
Moro-te Jodan Kei-tou-Uke

98.
Migi-Neko-Ashi-Dachi
Moro-te Jodan-Soto-Mawashi

102. (Kiai)
Migi Zenkutsu-Dachi
Moro-te Chudan-Nuki-te

99.
Migi Neko-Ashi-Dachi
Moro-te Shuto Gedan-Barai

102a. (side view)

100.
Migi Neko-Ashi-Dachi
Moro-te Kei-tou-Uke

103.
Hidari Zenkutsu-Dachi
Migi-Shuto
Hidari Hira-Nuki-te

(turn 180 degrees counter
clockwise)

100a. (side view)

104.
Hidari Zenkutsu-Dachi
Migi Gyaku-Shuto-Uke

213

105.
Yame

106a.
Kiotsuke

106b.
Rei

106c.

107.
Naore

Appendix

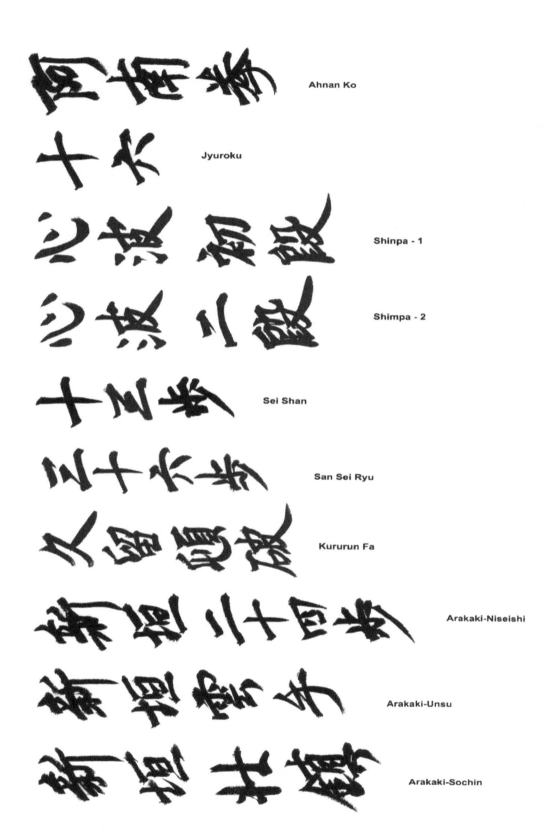

Ahnan Ko

Jyuroku

Shinpa - 1

Shinpa - 2

Sei Shan

San Sei Ryu

Kururun Fa

Arakaki-Niseishi

Arakaki-Unsu

Arakaki-Sochin

Itosu-Lohai

Matsumora-Lohai

Original Jion

WanSu

WanKwan

ChatanYara-Kushanku

Matsumura Passai

Yabu-Chinto

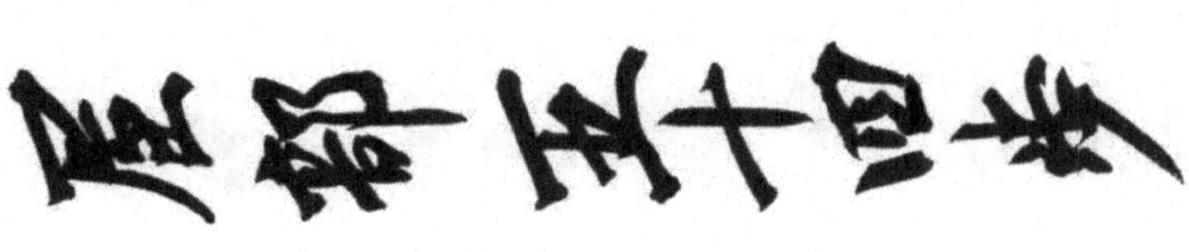

Yabu-Useshi

217

Back Row: George Kawamoto, unknown, Herbert Lee, Richard Lee
Front Row: Leroy Rodrigues, Peter Urban, Richard 'Biggie' Kim, unknown, Frank Haitsuka
Circa 1968

Leroy Rodrigues, Dianna Shu, Frank Barajas
Circa 1969

unknown, Johnny Pereira, Urbano Tejo, Richard 'Biggie' Kim, Diana Shu,
Daisy Chin, unknown, Frank Gaviola
Circa 1969

unknown, George Kawamoto, unknown, Frank Haitsuka,
Herbert Lee, Deanna Lee, Diane Moore, Leroy Rodrigues
Circa 1969

Nobu Kaji, Chester Chan, Leroy Rodrigues, Bernardo Mercado, Angel Lemus, Rick Clark
Circa 1994

Officials at table: Kjird, Yamaguchi, Kim, Nishiyama, Load and Hize Moore.

Right side representing Northern Calif.

1962

John Pereira, Leroy Rodrigues, Jerry Streeter, George Kawamoto, Clarence Lee, Rich Lee, Vince Cuoco, and Frank Yuen "China".

Left side representing Southern Calif.

Kaylor Adkins, James Yabe, Takashi Aoki, unknown, Ray Salky, and the last three is unknown.

1st North Cal vs. South Cal Karate Tournament 1962

Leroy Rodrigues and Hidetaka Nishiyama
Circa 1964

Back Row: unknown, Richard 'Biggie' Kim, Herbert Lee, Chuck Norris, Richard Lee, Duke Moore
Front Row: Johnny Pereira, Leroy Rodrigues, unknown
Circa 1965

ATAMA Cofounders:

Back Row: Leroy Rodrigues, Mike Cassazza, Marty McKowski, Johnny Pereira
Front Row: Hank Langley, Tim Flannigan, Mike Lipinski
Circa 1975

Johnny Pereira, Leroy Rodrigues, Clarence Lee
Circa 1985

Clarence Lee and Leroy Rodrigues, Circa 2012

Duke Moore
Vice President

Circa 1968

Herbert Lee
Tour. Director

Circa 1968

Lefty Nakayama
Advisor

Circa 1968

大日本武徳会空手教士
大東流合氣柔術七段

Richard 'Biggie' Kim, Circa 1968

Judges for the 2013 Fremont Shotokan Karate Traditional Black Belt Tournament

Back Row:
Al McGaughey, Steve McCann, Akihiro Omi, Leroy Rodrigues, Bernard Edwards, Ricardo Llewelyn, Jim Larkin Jr., Jon Keeling, Sue Miller, Joji Mercado, Lisa Cresta

Front Row:
Jay Castellano, Stuart Sakai, Ric Sherrod, Bernardo Mercado, Harry Imamura, Nobu Kaji

SHIN-KYU SHOTO-KAN KATA LIST

Shotokan kata	Shorinji-Ryu Equivalent		
	Shuri-te	Tomari-te	Naha-te
Tai-kyoku Shodan			
Hei-an, Sho-dan	Pin-an		*Goju-kata
Ni-dan			
San-dan			Gekisai
Yon-dan			
Go-dan			
Tekki, Sho-dan	Naihanchi		San-chin
Ni-dan			
San-dan			Sai-fa
			Sanseru
Bassai-dai	Matsumura-Passai		Kururun-fa
Bassai-sho	Passai-sho		Supa-rinpei
Kanku-dai	Kusanku-dai	Yara-Kusanku	
Kanku-sho	Kusanku-sho		
	Chibana-Kusanku		
Jion		Koryu-Jion	
Jitte		Jitte	
Jiin		Jiin	
Hangetsu			Seisan
Enpi		Wan-su	
Chin-te			Shinpa, Rinpa (Mabuni's)
Gan-kaku		Yabu-Chin-to	
Sochin			Arakaki-Sochin
Nijyushi-ho			Arakaki-Niseshi
Mei-kyo		Itosu-Lohai	
		Matsumora-Lohai	
Wan-kan		Wan-kuak	
Un-su			Arakaki-Unsu
Gojyushi-ho-dai			
Gojyushi-ho-sho	Yabu-Useshi		
			Juroku, Ananku (Mabuni's)
			Haku-tsuru

235

Dojo-Kun

1. **Seek Perfection of Character.**
   (Integrity)

2. **Be Faithful.**
   (Loyalty)

3. **Always Endeavor.**
   (Effort)

4. **Respect Others.**
   (Etiquette)

5. **Refrain from Violent Behavior.**
   (Control)

Originally written by
Gichin Funakoshi 1868 - 1957

Select Bibliography

Shigeru Egami, *The Heart of Karate-Do* (1976, Tokyo).

Keinosuke Enoeda, *Shotokan Karate: 5th Kyu to Black Belt* (1996, London).

Emil Farcas & John Corcoran, *The Overlook Martial Arts Dictionary* (1983, New York).

Jose M. Fraguas, *Karate Masters* (2001, Burbank).

Gichin Funakoshi, translated by Tsutomu Ohshima, *Karate-Do Kyohan: The Master Text* (1973, New York).

Hirokazu Kanazawa, *Shotokan Karate International Kata Vol.1* (1981, Tokyo).

Hirokazu Kanazawa, *Shotokan Karate International Kata Vol.2* (1982, Tokyo).

Hirokazu Kanazawa, *The Complete Kumite: Karate Fighting Techniques* (2004, Tokyo).

Richard 'Biggie' Kim, *The Weaponless Warriors: An Informal History of Okinawan Karate* (1974, Burbank).

Richard 'Biggie' Kim, *The Classical Man* (1982, Canada).

Steve McCann & Bernardo Mercado, *Karate Everyone, 2nd Edition* (2012, Winston-Salem).

Luis Bernardo Mercado, *Tsuku Kihon: Dynamic Kumite Techniques of Shotokan Karate, 2nd Edition* (2014, Bloomington).

Duke Moore, *Holistic Meditation: A Matter of Survival* (San Francisco).

Duke Moore, *The Self-Defense Syndrome of the Human Mind* (1979, San Francisco).

Masatoshi Nakayama, *Practical Karate Series* (1963, Tokyo).

Masatoshi Nakayama, *Dynamic Karate* (1966, Tokyo).

Masatoshi Nakayama, *Best Karate Series* (1977, Tokyo).

Hidetaka Nishiyama & Richard C. Brown, *Karate: The Art of "Empty Hand" Fighting* (Tokyo, 1959).

Masutatsu Oyama, *Vital Karate* (1967, San Francisco).

Mas Oyama, *Essential Karate* (1975, Tokyo).

Masutatsu Oyama, *Mastering Karate* (1966, New York).

Mayer H. Parry, *A Basic Glossary of Bujutsu* (1975, Scotland).

Elmar T. Schmeisser, Ph.D., *Advanced Karate-Do: Concepts, Techniques and Training Methods* (1994, Missouri).

John Sell, Unante: *The Secrets of Karate* (1995, Hollywood).

Shojiro Sugiyama, *25 Shotokan Kata* (1984, Chicago).

Peter Urban, *The Karate Dojo* (1967, Rutland).

Don Warrener, *20th Century Samurai: Richard 'Biggie' Kim 1917 – 2001* (2006, Hollywood).

Bernd W. Weiss, Ph.D. & Hilda O. Weiss, MBA. *Crime Fighters' Psychology* (2000, Calabasas)

Bernd W. Weiss, Ph.D., *Self Defense in Kata: Volume 1, Heian #1* (1998, Calabasas).

Bernd W. Weiss & Hilda Overstreet Weiss, *Self-Defense for Everybody* (1992, Calabasas).

Acknowledgment

Thank you to my wonderful wife of 34 years, Gale Trent Rodrigues.

Thanks

Thank you to the person who got me started in karate, Diane Marie Moore. She is also the mother of our two sons, Rico and Mike.

Thank you to my dedicated senior students and longtime instructors at *Shinkyu Shotokan Karate* (SSK) dojo:

Active at the SSK dojo –

Sue Miller, Chief Instructor

Nobu Kaji

Jason Leung

Patrick Dunleavy

Conrad Chu

Past SSK instructors residing elsewhere –

Elmar Schmeisser, North Carolina

Bernardo Mercado, Fremont Shotokan Karate dojo

Chester Chan, Oakland

Steve Ramirez, Brentwood

Mike Thomson, Cloverdale

Lisa Cresta, Elk Grove

Lita Tayao Zerbe, North Carolina

Steve Heard, Sacramento

Diana Cook, Vallejo

Much Appreciation

Thank you to Steve McCann, Chief Instructor at the *West Valley Shotokan Karate* dojo, for his unending support of the SSK dojo.

Thank you to Jon Keeling, Chief Instructor at the *Silicon Valley Shotokan Karate* dojo, for his many years of working as Chief Referee at the Annual Shinkyu Shotokan Karate Tournament.

Thank you to the *Hakua Kai* instructors for their friendship and support throughout the years:

Bernard Edwards, Edwards Karate in Foster City

Ric Sherrod, Sherrod's Karate Club in Daly City

Thank you to the *Northern California Karate League* (NCKL) for their support of Shinkyu Shotokan Karate events held throughout the years. Founding members are:

Steve McCann, West Valley College

Pete Rabbitt, DeAnza College

Dennis Clima, Santa Clara University

Joe Garcia, Santa Clara University

Thank you to the *Funakoshi Karate* dojo instructors:

Kenneth Funakoshi

Chet Kawashigi

Leonard Lafferty

Gary Cross

Les Haraguchi

Chronological History of Leroy Rodrigues

1938 - born in Waimeia Kauai, Hawaii.

1955 - joined U.S. Navy, stationed in Alameda, CA where he also trained as an amateur fly weight boxer.

1959 - moved to San Francisco.

1961 - began his martial arts training under Danzan-Ryu Jujitsu master teacher Duke Moore at the Market Street Dojo in San Francisco.

1961 - received Sho Dan from Duke Moore while Yoshiaki Ajari was teaching at the Dojo.

1962 - received 2nd Dan and was selected for the Northern California Kumite team for the 1st North Cal vs. South Cal Karate Tournament.

1963 - met JKA masters H. Nishiyama, T. Mikami and M. Mori at Duke Moore's Market Street Dojo.

1964 - began training with Richard 'Biggie' Kim, Dai-Nippon Butoku-Kai Representative, Shorinji-Ryu Karate and Okinawan Kobudo, Daito-Ryu Jujitsu master teacher at the Chinatown YMCA Dojo, in San Francisco, CA.

1961 to 1964 – Trained with Yoshiaki Ajari (Wado Ryu), Walter Todd (Shudokan), and Hidetaka Nishiyama (Shotokan) at Duke Moore's Market Street Dojo.

1967 - awarded 1st Place and Grand Champion of the International Karate Tournament, Long Beach, CA.

1968 – awarded 1st place in kata and 2nd place in kumite at the California Karate Championships.

1968 - started Karate program for the South San Francisco Parks and Recreation Department.

1975 - received 5th Dan in Karate and Kobudo from Richard 'Biggie' Kim.

1976 - began training with Shotokan teacher Chuck Okimura in San Jose, CA.

1980 - received 7th Dan from Duke Moore, Zen Budo-Kai while also training with Taigu C. Lee, Richard Lee and Peter Urban at Taraval Street Dojo, San Francisco, CA.

1981 - left Butoku-Kai; joined Goju-Ryu with master teacher Gosei Yamaguchi for one year.

1983 - formalized own dojo, Shinkyu Shotokan Karate (meaning: new and old style) teaching all Shotokan Kata from Chuck Okimura and Shorinji-Ryu Kata from Richard 'Biggie' Kim. Leroy Rodrigues is founder and Chief Instructor of the Shinkyu Shotokan Karate Dojo, where he continues training and teaching to maintain all new and old Kata.

1985 – original founding member of the American Martial Arts Teachers Association (ATAMA).

1988 - received 8th Dan from Duke Moore.

1994 - Co-Founder of The International Society of Okinawan Japanese Karate-Do (ISOK) with Dr. Bernd W. Weiss.

1998 - received 9th Dan from Duke Moore.

2013 - received 10th Dan from Taigu C. Lee.